GBENGA & JANET
ADEGBENRO

THE
SEVEN
SPIRITS
OF
God

TO OPERATE
ON THE THRONE

For further information or permission, contact:
Gbenga and Janet Adegbenro
Psalm138vs4@gmail.com
www.globalthronesministries.com

All scripture quotations are from the New King James Version of the Bible except otherwise stated

Editing: Alida Pretorius
Typesetting: Mona Gouws
Cover design: Mariaan Joubert

Printing and binding by:
Groep 7 Drukkers en Uitgewers (Pty) Ltd
www.groep7.co.za

Table of Contents

Dedication

The seven Spirits of God is dedicated to the Trinity – God the Father, the Son and the Holy Spirit.

> *"The Lord by wisdom founded the earth; by understanding He established the heavens; By His knowledge the depths were broken up, and clouds drop down the dew"*
>
> **Proverbs 3:19-20**

Acknowledgments

We owe our heartfelt gratitude always and forever to God Almighty, our faithful Heavenly Father, who gave us counsel in due season and instructed us to write this book and who baptised us with His seven Spirits to be a living witness to the greatness of His power on the planet.

We greatly appreciate our precious children Goodness, Mercy and Peace Adegbenro for giving us the enabling environment to practice all what is written in this book with them at the home front and for their support, understanding and prayers.

We are grateful to all the men and women of God who including my siblings who labored in prayers fervently until this book was published. May the Lord give you all an eternal great reward.

Our profound gratitude also goes to all our spiritual mentors, the men and women of God whose books have been a great spiritual resources to us and all the trained Throne Intercessors from the 2013 to 2020 set who have committed to training and practice of the operational principles in this book.

We greatly appreciate our Spirit-filled editor Alida Pretorius.

May you all be eternally rewarded by the Heaven of heavens in Jesus' powerful name.

About the book

Jesus Christ prevailed triumphantly and finished well by the seven horns' anointing and the seven Spirits of God all through His ministry on earth. He has equipped us with the same supernatural power and authority through the baptism of the seven Spirits of God for a high level of discernment and sensitivity to God's voice, guidance, counsel, instructions and directions for a victorious life on earth through His seven eyes which are the seven Spirits of God. As you prayerfully read the seven Spirits of God;

- Your spiritual antennae will tune in to discern the voice of God distinctly;

- You will experience a paradigm shift as your spiritual gifts and natural endowment will be ignited to manifest the glory of God and fulfill your kingdom destiny;

- You will understand the strategic operation of the seven Spirits of God and begin to operate in the supernatural realm by the power of the Holy Spirit;

- Your dreams and visions will become more vivid with clear interpretations to rule, reign, subdue kingdoms and fulfill your kingdom purpose on earth; and

- You will understand how to overcome all the storms of life as an overcomer in Christ Jesus.

Preface

God desires to communicate with us through all our senses and He wants our spiritual antennae to tune in to His frequency more finely so that we will be highly sensitive to His instructions, guidance and divine direction.

The Lamb takes the scroll

"And I saw in the right hand of Him who sat on the throne a scroll written inside and on the back, sealed with seven seals. Then I saw a strong angel proclaiming with a loud voice, "Who is worthy to open the scroll and to loose its seals?" And no one in heaven or on the earth or under the earth was able to open the scroll, or to look at it.

So I wept much, because no one was found worthy to open and read the scroll, or to look at it. But one of the elders said to me, "Do not weep. Behold, the Lion of the tribe of Judah, the Root of David, has prevailed to open the scroll and to loose its seven seals.

"And I looked, and behold, in the midst of the throne and of the four living creatures, and in the midst of the elders, stood a Lamb as though it had been slain, having seven horns and seven eyes, which are the seven

Spirits of God sent out into all the earth. Then He came and took the scroll out of the right hand of Him who sat on the throne."

Worthy Is the Lamb

Now when He had taken the scroll, the four living creatures and the twenty-four elders fell down before the Lamb, each having a harp, and golden bowls full of incense, which are the prayers of the saints. And they sang a new song, saying:

"You are worthy to take the scroll, And to open its seals; For You were slain, And have redeemed us to God by Your blood out of every tribe and tongue and people and nation, And have made us kings and priests to our God; And we shall reign on the earth."

Revelation 5: 1-10 (NKJV)

Revelation five is the authenticity of our Kingdom identity and the powerful weapon of our warfare as overcomers in Christ Jesus. The devil does not have any answer for Revelation 5 when you use this scripture as a legal evidence against the kingdom of darkness, and his tactical agenda to rule over your holy inheritance and steal your Kingdom destiny.

It establishes and authenticates our legal delegated authority over the kingdom of darkness. It authenticates our legal throne on earth and sets the boundaries of where to exercise our priesthood as God's representatives that are to rule, reign, subdue kingdoms and dominate the earth!

Neither Satan, nor the hosts in the first and second Heaven were able to open the scroll and open its 7 seals. Every creature in heaven and on the earth, under the earth and in the sea give glory, honour blessings and power to Him who sits on the throne, and to the Lamb who alone is worthy forever and ever! Therefore, no beasts, false prophets, demons, prognosticators, astrologers, principalities, sorcerers or witches have the power to steal your kingdom destiny because Jesus has prevailed!

The full details of our destiny as believers in Christ Jesus are only known to and controlled by the Lion of the tribe of Judah, **JESUS** who paid a great price with His blood and He alone was found worthy to open the scroll of our lives and to unfold the mysteries that are written in the book concerning us. We must pursue and seek to understand and fulfill these mysteries in due season and finish well before we depart to join the overcomers who have prevailed on the earth to sit upon the throne with Jesus, the King of kings (Revelation 5:7-9)

It is imperative to pray and ask the Lord to unlock our Kingdom destiny as it is written in the book concerning each one on earth. We must seek diligently to manifest what is written in the book concerning us and strive to finish well by the power of the fullness of the Holy Spirit.

The devil has no legal right to stop you from fulfilling your Kingdom destiny and inheriting the crowns of life and glory!

Operating in the Spirit

I heard the Lord say, "My people will prepare the way by returning to My ancient paths as well as operating in Zechariah 4:6. For it is only by being filled and led by My Spirit that My Kingdom plans will advance. Just as John the Baptist's message included a call to baptism for repentance, 'Prepare the way of the Lord, make His path straight!' My people need to be filled with My Spirit in order to be carriers of My glory."

The Lord is calling us to walk in close fellowship with His Holy Spirit and to only move on His command. **We will only see God's plans advance as we submit to His leadership.** The Lord is filling His people with His Spirit so they will be equipped to powerfully transform their spheres of influence. We are called to follow the example of Jesus and only do what we see the Father doing. As our hearts are aligned with the Father's and as we are led by the Spirit, we will bring glory to the name of Jesus.

The Lord is calling people back to the ancient paths. He is calling people to take the narrow path which is the path of holiness, humility and surrender. There is a higher path but few are willing to count the cost. God's glory will be seen in a greater measure in the days ahead through the ones that have been separated out, refined, and prepared to carry what God will pour out in and through them. It is only the consecrated priests that will be able to carry the glory and restore the glory of God among the nations of the earth.

> "...Not by might nor by power, but by My Spirit,' says the LORD of hosts."
> ### Zechariah 4:6 (NKJV)

> "I indeed baptise you with water unto repentance, but He who is coming after me is mightier than I, whose sandals I am not worthy to carry. He will baptize you with the Holy Spirit and fire."
> ### Matthew 3:11 (NKJV)

> "Thus says the LORD: 'Stand you in the ways and see, and ask for the old paths, where the good way is, and walk in it; then you will find rest for your souls."
> ### Jeremiah 6:16. (NKJV)

Outpouring of God's Glory

The Lord went on to say, "My glory will be poured out through refined, renewed and prepared vessels. Now is the time to be ready. Now is the time to prepare the way. The call to prepare the way is not just for individuals but for nations. An awakening is upon My Church, and as My Church awakens and arises, destinies over nations will be reclaimed. Prepare the way, for a great outpouring of My glory is coming to the earth."

Dr. Janet Bolaji Adegbenro
Global Thrones Ministries
Pretoria, South Africa
June 2, 2020

Note: All the Bible verse references in this book comes from the New King James Version (NKJV), unless otherwise specified.

Comments

You have asked for my impressions on your book. For a few months now God kept saying to me: Learn to recognise My voice immediately, so you know when it's Me speaking – and more importantly, when it is NOT Me. I found strong confirmation in your book when you repeatedly mentioned our spiritual antennae being tuned into God's frequency. I now realise that He means to teach all His children about this. I think it's incredibly important to know exactly what His voice sounds like and how it feels when He speaks, so that we can ignore any other voices that are not from Him.

I have actually made a promise to myself to use your book as a prolonged Bible study and take one Spirit at a time and study it intensely. It's a lovely guide on how to get to know God in a deeper, more serious way and also to dedicate everything I do to Him – because in concentrating on **His seven Spirits**, I will be tuning my entire life on all levels into His frequency. I will also be able to use His influence to step into my holy calling that He has for me. I think this book is more of a workbook and a companion book to get intimate with God through His seven Spirits in a practical way.

Alida Pretorius, Pretoria, South Africa

Seven Spirits of God Workbook

The subject matter for this book is spiritually dense and lends itself to deeper study. We have therefore decided to create a workbook to help you explore and experience the seven Spirits in a supernatural way and get to know God more intimately while you study His word. This will include a guided Bible study and assignment for each Spirit, along with some practical activities to ensure your learning has a lasting impact on the development of your Kingdom identity to operate on the Thrones on earth. Look out for this exciting development soon!

~ **Alida Pretorius, Pretoria, South Africa**

Chapter One

Restoration of God's Kingdom Glory on the Seven Thrones

The vision of an open-roofed car

I asked God what was burning in His heart that I must be busy with in the following year as we cross over to the New Year. The Lord answered by showing me an open roofed car occupied by men dressed in military uniform. The car was hovering above the ground. In the centre of the car was a tall image covered with fresh blood from head to toe.

I started shivering when I saw this vision and I asked the Lord who are these people and what is their mission on earth? I heard the Lord say in my spirit: "These are the angels of restoration in a mobile throne whom I have sent ahead to restore My glory upong the 7 thrones on the earth among the youth, families, marriages, babies, kings, queens, governors and nations of the whole world."

He said further: "My glory must be fully restored on the earth and this is what is burning in My heart. These angels have gone ahead to assist My glory carrier to restore My glory among the nations, that My glory may cover the earth again as waters cover the seas!"

The Seven Thrones to Operate on the Earth

"And have made us kings and priests to our God, And we shall reign on the earth."

Revelation 5:10

"Here is the mind which has wisdom, The seven heads are seven mountains on which the woman sits."

Revelation 17:9

These seven thrones are the seven mountains of influence in the society where all kingdom believers as priests and kings must rule, reign, subdue the kingdom of darkness and enforce the will of God upon their throne as it is being done in heaven.

These seven thrones are:

- Government Throne
- Education Throne
- Business and Market Throne
- Media and Technology Throne
- Arts and Culture Throne
- Religion Throne
- Family and Health Throne

God Almighty expects all creation to manifest His glory daily on earth with the gifts He has endowed to us. *The ultimate purpose of a human being on earth is to reveal the glory of God.*

The ultimate agenda of the devil is to steal and destroy the glory of God on the earth and in the lives of all creation. This is why everyone needs the revelation knowledge of their kingdom purpose and their individual role in restoring the glory of God upon the earth. The battle is real on a daily basis!

Believers today are ignorant of the fierce battle and of their Kingdom destiny and purpose on earth. This happens when believers do not have a revelation knowledge of who they are and the usefulness of the keys of the Kingdom that were delivered into our hands as believers in Christ Jesus and king-priests to rule, reign, subdue the kingdom of darkness and dominate the earth to the glory of God the Father.

"The keys of the house of David I will lay on his shoulder; so he shall open, and no one shall shut; and he shall shut, and no one shall open, I will fasten him as a peg in a secure place, And he will become a glorious Throne to his father's house. They will hang on him all the glory of his father's house, the offspring and the posterity, all vessels of small quantity, from the cups to all the pitchers".

Isaiah 22:22-24

The restoration of the Kingdom glory is absolutely the work of the Holy Spirit. It is a critical issue that the ruler of this present world, Satan, is really waging war against the Kingdom of God and he will fight it till the end without relenting or giving up. We have the consolation that the battle is not ours and that it has already been won.

Jesus Christ paid the price with His blood. He was led by the fullness of the seven Spirits of God and not by His flesh; His flesh was crucified but the Holy Spirit cannot be killed. Jesus Christ was buried but the Holy Spirit was active in the grave. A war was waged inside the grave with the devil who had power over death. Jesus Christ, by the Holy Spirit, led captivity captive, destroyed the power of darkness and collected the keys of death and hell from the ruler of this present world because He was filled with the fullness of the Holy Spirit. This is the reason why the grave could not hold Him. The Holy Spirit is the spirit of light and truth and in Him there is no darkness. His light shines in the darkness and darkness cannot comprehend Him. Darkness can only exist where there is no light.

After Jesus Christ collected the keys of the Kingdom and of death and hell from the devil, He destroyed the veil that he, the ruler of this world has been using to cover mankind. He gave us the keys and the grace according to the measure of His gifts to operate these keys appropriately before He ascended up on high, to present His blood in the third heaven, sitting now at the right hand of the Father interceding with the Holy Spirit for us and waiting until the ruler of this world will be made our footstool.

> *"But to each of us grace was given according to the measure of Christ's gift. "Therefore, he says: "when He ascended on high, He led captivity captive, And gave gifts to men." Now this, "He ascended" what does it mean but that He also first descended into the lower parts of the earth? He who descended is also the One who ascended far above all the heavens, that He might fill all things." And He Himself gave some to be apostles, some prophets, some evangelists, and some pastors and teachers, for the equipping of the saints for the work of ministry, for the edifying of the body of Christ, till we all come to the unity of the faith and of the knowledge of the Son of God, to a perfect man, to the measure of the stature of the fullness of Christ."*

Ephesians 4:7-13

We should constantly rejoice in this, because the battle has already been won. The same power of the Holy Spirit in agreement with the Father that worked in our Lord Jesus Christ inside the grave and destroyed the devil and his power over death, is still the Holy Spirit that lives in us today! We must now utilise the power of the Holy Spirit to win the war inside and outside to restore our Kingdom inheritance and take back our nations and kingdoms from the ruler of this present world by fire. We must reclaim the Kingdom with power and force because the devil will never let go or give up!

The battle for our Kingdom inheritance has been won and the keys and power of the Holy Spirit have been given unto us. He is active in us and living inside of us. We need to understand this perfectly and use these keys to reign, rule, subdue, dominate and possess all our Kingdom benefits in full. Jesus said: "Because l go to my Father, greater work than l did you will do. If l do not go the Holy Spirit of promise will not come. When the Holy Spirit comes He will teach you all things. Greater works you will do because l go to my Father."

The level of the baptism of the fullness of the seven Spirits of God in you will determine the measure of the grace of God that will be released unto you. It is the Holy Spirit who releases grace. The Holy Spirit releases the measure of grace we need daily to operate our potential and use the gifts of God in us to actualise and fulfill His Kingdom purposes.

Declaration of God's glory

> "The heavens declare the glory of God; and the firmament shows His handiwork. Day unto day utters speech, and night unto night reveals knowledge. There is no speech nor language where their voice is not heard."

Psalm 19:1-3

> "Even every one that is called by my name; for I have created him for my glory, I have formed him; yea; I have made him."

Isaiah 43:7

"Everyone who is called by My name, whom I have created for My glory. I have formed him, yes, I have made him." All creation was created to reveal the glory of God. The sun, the moon, the sky and the stars. There is glory assigned to the sun, the moon and the stars and each of them must reveal the glory of God in their due times and seasons – like the rest of creation.

All human beings that God created are to reveal the glory of God in their different times and seasons through the manifold grace of God. We are created to be God's glory carrier on the earth.

The glory carriers are consecrated vessels that are separated for the Master's use. You cannot carry God's glory with sins in your life! If you are under the bondage of corruption, sins, iniquities and faulty ancestral foundations, you cannot carry the glory of God and manifest His glory among the nations.

"For all have sinned and fall short of the glory of God."

Romans 3:23

Every sin, iniquity and unrighteousness makes man fall short of the glory of God. The glory was originally stolen from the Garden of Eden because of disobedience and God Himself, by His wisdom came in a human body with a soul and a spirit through Jesus Christ to pay the expensive price and make the necessary sacrifice for the remission of our sin and the restoration of His glory and power to His people.

Great awareness is being created in these last days for the restoration of the glory of God in people's lives, the Church, families, the youth, marriages, kingdoms and nations. Satan is fully aware that his time is very short and he is in a great hurry to steal, kill and destroy the glory of God's kingdom on earth and the inheritance of the saints in Christ Jesus.

The main reason why the battle is becoming fiercer in individual lives, families and marriages, causing many cases of divorce even in the church, is because Satan is aware of the fact that he has such little time left.

God, in His infinite mercy, has also released His innumerable army of angels of restoration that excels in strength and will assist the saints in the process of the restoration of God's glory to cover the earth as water covers the sea, before the return of the Lord Jesus Christ.

The throne of glory

The throne of glory is the inheritance of the saints. The saints need the baptism of the fullness of the seven Spirits of God to prevail against the gates of hell and dominate their inheritance to the glory of God's name.

> *"The bows of the mighty men are broken, and those who stumbled are girded with strength. Those who were full have hired themselves out for bread, and the hungry have ceased to hunger. Even the barren has borne seven, and she who has many children has become feeble. The Lord kills and makes alive; He brings down to the grave and brings up. The Lord makes poor and makes rich; He brings low and lifts up. He raises the poor from the dust. And lifts the beggar from the ash heap. To set them among princes. And make them inherit the Throne of Glory."*
>
> ### 1 Samuel 2:4-8

"For the Lord God is a sun and shield; The Lord will give grace and glory; No good thing will He withhold from those who walk uprightly".

Psalm 84:11

Manifesting God's glory

"Awake my glory! Awake lute and harp! I will awaken the dawn. I will praise You, o Lord, among the peoples; I will sing to You among the nations. For Your mercy reaches unto the heavens And your truth unto the clouds. Be exalted, O God above the heavens; Let Your glory be above all the earth."

Psalm 57:8-11

The glory of God is the gifts and the power of God that work within us. The glory of God upon us is our inheritance, is the fragrance of our life, the substance that comes out of our life to impact creation positively, and bring dispensational transformation to people's lives, kingdoms and nations.

Your glory is God's value in your life, which was stolen originally from the Garden of Eden. Satan was jealous of the glory that was given to man through Adam and Eve. He deceived Eve and persuaded her to commit sin. The devil knew that God would never go back on His word. Where there sin, there will be a consequence because God will never approve of sin. Satan made Adam and Eve sin against God and fall short of the glory of God that was freely given to man to enjoy the presence of God. He stole the gifts of God's splendor, beauty, awesomeness and glory from them.

Adam and Eve were covered by the glory of God in the Garden of Eden. They were naked but they did not know because the glory of God's kingdom covered their nakedness.

"And they were both naked, the man and his wife, and were not ashamed."

Genesis 2:25

This is the season to arise from obscurity and be resolute and determined to shake off every weight, sin, unrighteousness and unnecessary burden that so easily robs you of the fire of God.

As soon as you arise and remain determined to shine forth the glory of God, the Lord will arise also over you. He will release the measure of grace, abundance and mercy you need to shine forth His glory to the point of bringing the gentiles to your light. God expects creation to reveal His glory according to what is written in the scroll concerning His people in the court of heaven.

"But to each one of us grace was given according to the measure of Christ's gift. Therefore He says; when He ascended on high, He led captivity captive, And gave gifts to men."

Ephesians 4:7-8

When you are at the centre of the will of God and revealing His glory, He will reveal His mysteries to you the more and take you to a higher level where you will recognise and hear His voice distinctly. God relates intimately with those who carry His purpose jealously and manifest His glory and those who live only for His pleasure.

Those who follow on to understand the seasons of their lives and fulfil their purpose will receive deep revelation from the Lord continually and they will never stumble because God will watch over their lives jealously. Their lives will be precious in sight of the Lord.

Daniel's focus and his ultimate life goal was to reveal the glory of God. He faced the lion's den without flinching and God sent His angels to guard him and shut the mouths of the lions. The king made a decree to glorify God's name and made His name famous. Shortly after this, God began to reveal deep mysteries of what will happen at the end time to Daniel, which gave Daniel a prophetic insight into the end times.

Esther manifested the glory of God as a young Queen and God glorified Himself in her life.

This is the season to get rid of all your faulty mindsets, wrong associations, false altars, ancestral deceptions and faulty foundations which open the gates of your life to the kingdom of darkness.

And be determined to shine forth the glory of God so you can receive the fullness of the Holy Spirit and the Throne grace at every season to shine forth the glory of God in your lifetime!

The glory carriers

"Arise and shine; for your light has come! And the glory of the Lord is risen upon you. For behold, the darkness shall cover the earth, And deep darkness the people; But the Lord will arise over you, And His glory will be seen upon you!"

Isaiah 60:1-2

"For I consider that the sufferings of this present time are not worthy to be compared with the GLORY which shall be revealed in us. For the earnest expectation of the creation eagerly waits for the revealing of the sons of God. For the creation was subjected to futility, not willingly, but because of Him who subjected it in hope, because the creation itself will be delivered from the bondage of corruption into the glorious liberty of the children of God".

Romans 8:19-21

Those who will carry the glory of God must be filled with the fullness of the seven Spirits of God in these last days. Only the carriers of God's glory, who have been delivered from the bondage of corruption and have crossed over to the glorious liberty of the sons of God, will be able to transform the world of sin.

After Paul declared that the law of the spirit of life has set us free from the law of sin and death, he described the spirit-filled life as a life that carries the glory of God with liberty in the spirit, because the Holy Spirit empowers and helps us to manifest the glory of God.

"I beseech you therefore, brethren, by the mercies of God, that you present your bodies a living sacrifice, holy, acceptable to God, which is your reasonable service. And do not be conformed to this world, but be transformed by the renewing of your mind, that you may prove what is that good and acceptable and perfect will of God."

Romans 12:1-2

- The glory carriers must lay aside every weight that locks the Holy Spirit out of their lives.

- The glory carriers must present themselves as a living sacrifice, holy and acceptable unto the Lord.

- The glory carriers must be disciplined, committed to doing the will of God in all things and at every point in life.

- The glory carriers must be ready to cleanse and circumcise their hearts with purity.

- The glory carriers must always walk in the Spirt so they will not fulfill the lust of the flesh.

- The glory carriers must consecrate themselves wholly to the service of God.

- The glory carriers must be focused with an eagle's view – not easily distracted and complacent.

- The glory carriers must set their faces like a flint, not compromising but always speak the truth from a pure heart.
- The glory carriers must be prepared and always ready to be among the overcomers who will sit upon the throne with Jesus at last.

"I say then; walk in the Spirit, and you shall not fulfil the lust of the flesh. For the flesh lusts against the Spirit, and the Spirit against the flesh; and these are contrary to one another, so that you do not do the things that you wish. But if you are led by the Spirit, you are not under the law."

Galatians 5:16

"It is the Spirit who gives life; the flesh profits nothing. The words that I speak to you are Spirit, and they are life."

John 6:63

"For as many as are led by the spirit of God, these are sons of God."

Romans 8:14

16

NOTES

....
....
....
....
....
....
....
....
....
....
....
....
....
....
....
....
....
....

Chapter Two

God's Seven Spirits for the Overcomers

Jesus Christ overcame, by the sacrifice of His blood and commands the same power to us, to prevail and be among the overcomers at the end as He Himself overcame!

He lived like we are living now, He passed through all we are passing through presently, yet He did not commit any sin. *He prevailed by the seven horns' anointing and the seven Spirits of God,* He was qualified to take the scroll from the hand of He who sat upon the Throne. He paid the price, He suffered and died a shameful death in order to take back the keys of the Kingdom, to dominate our inheritance to the glory of His name.

He promised all these benefits to the overcomers who lived a consecrated life on earth and are faithful to the end. Those who also lay hold on His promises, those who understand their Kingdom identity and have a revelation of the benefits for the overcomers who paid the price like Jesus did and prevailed against the gates of hell, and subdue the kingdom of darkness by the power and fullness of His seven Spirits and manifest His glory on earth!

In these last days, the demonstration of the power of God with signs and wonders will not only be by the anointing but by the manifestation of the glory of God's Kingdom.

Those who are baptised with the seven Spirits of God will be empowered to prevail against the gates of hell and conquer death and hell as Jesus Christ Himself did.

The saints of God that will be among the overcomers at last must first rule and reign on the earth as king-priests through the baptism of the fullness of the seven Spirits of God.

> *"And the seventh angel sounded; and there were great voices in heaven, saying, The kingdoms of this world are become the kingdoms of our Lord, and of His Christ; and he shall reign for ever and ever."*
> ### Revelation 11:15

The seven benefits for the overcomers are:

1) Power over the nations

> *"And he who overcomes, and keeps My works until the end, to him I will give power over the nations".*
> ### Revelation 2:26

"He shall rule them with a rod of iron; they shall be dashed to pieces like the potter's vessels, as I also have received from My Father, and I will give him the morning star". He who has an ear, let him hear what the Spirit says to the churches."

Revelation 2:27-29

Believers in Christ Jesus who are baptised with the fullness of the seven Spirits of God like Jesus will be able to prevail against the kingdom of darkness and subdue the powers and principalities. He has delegated the same power and authority unto us by the power of His Holy Spirit to overcome and prevail against the kingdom of darkness.

Those who are filled with the fullness of the 7 Spirits of God will receive the Nations as an inheritance.

"Ask of Me, and I will give You The nations for Your inheritance, and the ends of the earth for Your possession."

Psalm 2:8

2) The hidden manna

God is so deep and no man can know the depth of His knowledge. The hidden manna is one of the inheritance and mysterious food reserved only for the Overcomers, those who have rule on the earth with the 7 Spirits of God and prevailed.

"He who has an ear, let him hear what the Spirit says to the churches. To him who overcomes I will give some of the hidden manna to eat.

Revelation 2:17

3) A new name

All kingdom believers that lived on the earth and rule, reign, subdued the kingdom of darkness and dominate the earth through the baptism of the seven spirits of God and prevailed like Jesus Christ prevailed by the baptism of the seven horns anointing and the seven spirits of God, they will receive a New name which the mouth of the Almighty God will name and will only be revealed to the believer who overcame and received the new name! This is amazing!

"And I will give him a white stone, and on the stone a new name written which no one knows except him who receives it."

Revelation 2:17

"He who overcomes, I will make him a pillar in the temple of My God, and he shall go out no more, I will write on him the name of My God and the name of the city of My God, the New Jerusalem which comes down out of heaven from My God, and I will write on him My new name. He who has an ear, let him hear what the Spirit says to the churches."

Revelation 3:12-13

4) The tree of life

The kingdom believer that engaged and utilize the seven spirits of God on earth to manifest God's glory and fulfil his/her kingdom destiny on the earth, will eat out of the tree of life and be like God whose image we were originally made. It is so amazing that Adam and Eve at the Garden of Eden were prevented from eaten this tree of life so they will not be like God and not able to taste death forever!

> *"He who has an ear, let him hear what the Spirit says to the churches. To him who overcomes I will give to eat from the tree of life, which is in the midst of the Paradise of God."*
>
> ## *Revelation 2:7*

5) Sitting upon the throne

The kingdom believer who are baptized by the seven spirits of God on the earth and were able to rule as kings and priests who established the kingdom of God in the heart of all people and manifest the glory of His kingdom will sit upon the throne with the Lord Jesus Christ in heaven! This is glorious! This has always be a spiritual motivation and encouragement for me to move on to perfection and forgetting all the pains, affliction, challenges, and despair that might come my way in this kingdom life journey, knowing fully that soon and very soon I am going to sit upon the throne with the Lord Jesus Christ.

*"To him who overcomes I will grant to sit with Me on
My Throne, as I also overcame and sat down with My
Father on His Throne. He who has an ear, let him hear
what the Spirit says to the churches."*

Revelation 3:21-22

6) Clothed with white garments

*"He who overcomes shall be clothed in white garments,
and I will not blot out his name from the Book of Life;
but I will confess his name before My Father and before
His angels. He who has an ear let him hear what the
Spirit says to the churches."*

Revelation 3:5-6

The white garment and the attire for the Saints that the 24
elders are putting on, will be given to the Overcomes that
prevailed by the 7 Spirits of God on the earth.

7) Shall not be hurt by the second death

*"He that has an ear, let him hear what the Spirit said
to the churches; He that overcomes shall not be hurt of
the second death."*

Revelation 2:12

It is amazing that those who are baptized with the 7 Spirits of
God and lived a righteous life on earth will be among the
Overcomers who will not partake of the second death but will

only sleep and wakeup to live an eternal life with Jesus on His Throne.

NOTES

....

....

....

....

....

....

....

....

....

....

....

....

....

....

....

....

....

....

....

Chapter Three

The Seven Spirits of God

"And the spirit of the LORD shall rest on him, the spirit of wisdom and understanding, the spirit of counsel and might, the spirit of knowledge and of the fear of the LORD".

Isaiah 11:2

THE SEVEN SPIRITS OF GOD

The Seven Spirits of God is for Service

The seven Spirits of God comes through the glorification of the Lord and is for service for guidance, direction and divine leadership. When you are guided and led by the Spirit of the Lord, you are a child of God and a Kingdom citizen. The fullness of the Holy Spirit of God guarantees your sonship and gives you peace of mind in serving Him and fulfilling your Kingdom destiny.

> *"For as many as are led by the Spirit of God, these are sons of God."*
>
> ### Romans 8:14

The seven Spirits of God are sent to believers to maximize their potential and fulfill their Kingdom destiny on earth. The seven Spirits of God gives light and proper guidance to be where God wants you to be at the right time. As many that are baptised by the seven Spirits of God are under the leadership of the Holy Spirit and are influenced by the Holy Spirit to be great on earth and dominate their Kingdom inheritance.

> *"And shall make him of quick understanding in the fear of the LORD: and he shall not judge after the sight of his eyes, neither reprove after the hearing of his ears:"*
>
> ### Isaiah 11:3

The seven Spirits of the Lord impart you with the Spirit of truth that only hears directly from God because He is God living inside of us.

The seven Spirits of God subdue darkness

The anointing that comes from the baptism of the Holy Spirit breaks the yoke of the devil and sets us free to manifest the glory of God.

The light that shines through the 7 spirits of God is very strong and deep. The rays of the light of the countenance of the 7 eyes of God are very powerful, it destroys darkness and exposes hidden things and darkness cannot comprehend the light like a burning fire.

> *"And He will destroy on this mountain the surface of the covering cast over all people, and the veil that is spread over all nations. He will swallow up death forever, and the Lord God will wipe away tears from all faces; the rebuke of His people He will take away from all the earth; for the Lord has spoken."*
>
> ### Isaiah 25:7-8
>
> *"It shall come to pass in that day that his burden will be taken away from your shoulder, and his yoke from your neck, and the yoke will be destroyed because of the anointing oil."*

Isaiah 10:27

The seven Spirits of God tune in spiritual antennae

The baptism of the seven Spirits of God brings strength upon your spiritual antennae, and tunes the spiritual antennae to be able to see clearly, and discern with foresight. You will be able to pick up instant messages from the throne room of grace.

> *"But my horn You have exalted like a wild Ox; I have been anointed with fresh oil."*
>
> **Psalm 92:10**

Seven Spirits of God to dominate your Kingdom inheritance

The Kingdom of God is full of benefits and is the everlasting inheritance of the saints of God. The baptism of the seven Spirits of God empowers you to dominate all the benefits of the Kingdom of God to the glory of God's name.

> *"But the saints of the Most High shall receive the kingdom, and possess the kingdom forever, even forever and ever.*
>
> **Daniel 7:18**

"Do not fear, little flock for it is your Father's good pleasure to give you the kingdom."
Luke 12:32

"Blessed be the Lord, who daily loads us with benefits, the God of our salvation"
Psalms 68:19

Seven Spirits of God to deal with Gates

Gates represent access to authority, the Throne and the seat of power. The king has a throne at the gates. The elders often sit at the gates to make decisions and pass judgement. Gates are spiritual. Gates does not move, but the plan and God's expectation is that the Church must smash the gates of Hell. Gates are places where important decisions are taken.

Strongmen can be at gates in a city or nation as gatekeepers. Important decisions that involve life and death are taken at the gates. Businesses are established at the gates. Elders and Prophets of God stood at the gates of the city to make declarations from the Lord. Kings sat at the gates to dispense judgement.

"For a Spirit of justice to him who sits in judgement, And for strength to those who turn back the battle at the gate".
Isaiah 28:6

"You shall appoint judges and officers in all your gates, which the LORD your God gives you, according to your tribes, and they shall judge the people with judgement"

Deuteronomy 16:18.

Gates are Spiritual

Gates are powerful forces and supernatural entities that give access to the possessions of an everlasting inheritance.

Gates are significant phenomena in life, which need special understanding to move to the next level in life. God gave Abraham a promise in Genesis that he will possess the gates of his enemy and dominate his inheritance. Jesus also promised the disciples that He would give them the keys of the Kingdom, and that the gates of Hell shall not prevail against His church.

"That in blessing I will bless thee, and in multiplying I will multiply thy seed as the stars of the heaven and as the sand which is upon the sea shore; and thy seed shall possess the gate of his enemies."

Genesis 22:17

"And I also say to you that you are Peter, and on this rock I will build My church, and the gates of Hell shall not prevail against it."

Matthew 16:18

A gate is a doorway to authority. A gate is an entry point and departure point. A gate is a major element that determines the level of your possessions and productivity. A gate will not move without the right KEY! Little wonder that Jesus emphasized consecration in **Psalm 24:3-6** before He dealt with gates in **verses 7-10** for Him to be able to move and complete His Redemptive assignment!

"Who shall ascend into the hill of the Lord? Or who shall stand in his holy place? He that hath clean hands, and a pure heart; who hath not lifted up his soul unto vanity, nor sworn deceitfully, He shall receive the blessing from the Lord, and righteousness from the God of his salvation. This is the generation of them that seek him that seek thy face, O Jacob."

Psalm 24:3-6

There are gates that must be lifted in your life before you can actually access the throne of grace and fulfil your Kingdom destiny. Jesus had to deal with different gates and ancient doors before He could collect the keys of the Kingdom, and access the legal authority and power that He handed over to as many that believe in Him and accepted Him as their personal Lord and Saviour. We must use the keys to rule, reign, subdue principalities and powers in high places and dominate the earth and restore His glory.

> *"Lift up your heads, O ye gates; and be ye lift up, ye everlasting doors; and the King of glory shall come in. Who is this King of glory? The Lord strong and mighty, the Lord mighty in battle. Lift up your heads, O ye gates; even lift them up, ye everlasting doors; and the King of glory shall come in. who is this King of glory? The Lord of hosts, he is the King of glory."*
> ### Psalm 24:7-10

Gates can hear the spoken word because they are spiritual entities. Jesus was full of the seven spirits and seven horns anointing, He ordered the gates to be lifted with the authority and power of His word for Him to gain access to fulfil His redemptive purpose on the earth.

Types of Gates

There are different types of gates mentioned in the word of God with significant characteristics. There are physical, spiritual, commercial, political and institutional gates. We have to discern the gates in our cities and where they are located by using the power of the fullness of the seven spirits of God. We need to discern the strongmen and the gatekeepers that operate at these gates through the spirit of understanding. Gates have security guards that give signals to those strongmen that operate at the gates. We need the fullness of the spirit of divine wisdom and the keys of the Kingdom to deal with gates. Every satanic false altar raised in the market places, institutions, road junctions, the city entrances, hospitals and the nation's boarders are gates of Hell where the souls of men are tied and blood sacrifice is being made regularly with demonic activities going on at the gates.

Gates are significant in the fulfilment of kingdom destiny and possessing your possession to manifest the glory of God's kingdom upon the Throne.

David assigned gate keepers towards the end of 1 Chronicles Chapter 26, men who were full of the seven spirits of God as the gate keepers who understand what to do at the gate with wisdom and the spirit of counsel to man the gates.

"Among these were the divisions of the gatekeepers, among the chief men, having duties just like their brethren, to serve in the house of the LORD. And they cast lots for each gate, the small as well as the great, according to their father's house. The lots for the east gate fell to Shelemiah. Then they cast lots for his son

34

Zechariah, a wise counselor, and his lot came out for the North Gate.

The Seven Spirits of God enable us to rule on earth

"And have made us kings and Priests to our God; And we shall reign on the earth."

Revelation 5:10

The baptism of the seven Spirits of God empowers us and gives us the boldness to rule and subdue the kingdom of darkness and establish the Kingdom of our God on earth and His will as it is being done on earth. The seven Spirit of the Lord mandates us for position. It teaches us about our kingdom dominion and how to exercise our power, sonship and rulership on earth to the glory of God.

Strategic Prayer Counsels

Pray for the baptism of the 7 Spirits of the Lord upon your life:

1) Lord, baptise me with the fullness of the Godhead, which is the fullness of the **HOLY SPIRIT** and the spirit of the **GRACE of God.**

2) Lord, baptise me with the spirit of **WISDOM** to come to the place of prominence in life and reach the potential that God has created in me. Foolishness is the opposite of wisdom and it kills and destroys destiny.

3) Lord, baptise me with the spirit of **UNDERSTANDING.** to comprehend the voice of God.

4) Lord, baptise me with the spirit of **COUNSEL** to understanding the mind of Christ for right direction and the ability to make the right choices.

5) Lord, baptise me with the spirit of **MIGHT to have the** strength of character, correct focus and the skill for excellence.

6) Lord, baptise me with the spirit of **KNOWLEDGE.** to have ability to think critically and divergently, to have clear foresight, to know the mind of Christ, and quick to find solutions to problems.

7) Lord, baptise me with the spirit of the **FEAR OF GOD,** to reject evil and choose the right way.

NOTES

....
....
....
....
....
....
....
....
....
....
....
....
....
....
....
....
....
....
....

Chapter Four
The Seven Eyes of God

"And from the Throne proceeded lightning, thundering, and voices. Seven lamps of fire were burning before the Throne, which are the seven Spirits of God.

"Before the Throne there was a sea of glass, like crystal and in the midst of the Throne, were four living creatures full of eyes in front and in the back.

"The first living creature was like a Lion, the second living creature was like a calf, the third living creature had a face like a man, and the fourth living creature was like a flying eagle.

"The four living creatures, each having six wings, were full of eyes around and within. And they do not rest day or night. Saying Holy, holy, holy, Lord God almighty, who was and is and is to come!"

Revelation 4:5-8

The four living creatures had eyes on and all around their bodies and within. They would constantly see new sides and facets of the Lord Jesus – His beauty, splendor and glory. His majesty and holiness would radiate and manifest in new ways all the time, and these four living creatures would be in constant awe and wonder. Whenever they saw something about Jesus, they would move in a new way. *Their VISION affected their MISSION. Their SIGHT influenced their MIGHT.*

What you see affects your behavior and your sense of judgement! The four living creatures have eyes within themselves and many eyes in their front and at their back. Our inner eyes are the eyes of our spirit man, which is a significant and profound concept. When your spirit eyes are closed, you are already covered with darkness. What you will see will only be physical and you will not be able to see spiritual things as a divine personality.

When your inner eyes are opened, you will be able to see clearly with spiritual foresight. You will see the vision of God's Kingdom and you will discern the intent of the heart of God

It is imperative as believer in Christ Jesus to have your spirit eyes opened in order to be able to see clearly and do the will of God on earth as it is being done in heaven.

You cannot possess what you cannot see clearly. That is why God told Abraham to go and view the land and as far as he could see clearly, he would possess. We need a clear vision, like the eyes of an eagle to be able to dominate our Kingdom inheritance.

Whatever you don't see may be impossible to possess. What you see with your eyes will leave a bigger impression upon your heart than what you hear. What you see clearly in the spirit will spur you to action and move you to the point of manifestation.

You will not go too far if you cannot see clearly. When you possess clear vision, you will experience a definite call to action. There is, at many times, no movement because there is no **VISION**, therefore the people perish. Too many have perished because they did not possess **KINGDOM VISION**.

In these last days, there will be an outpouring of more of the fullness of the seven Spirits of the Lord, and it will impart His people with unprecedented revelation! The Lord will give clear vision and clarity of sight into the brightness of His kingdom glory so that you can properly soar and propel forward into your Kingdom destiny.

The 7 eyes of God and the 7 Spirits of God move hand-in-hand. It is a marriage and a synchronised partnership.

The Seven Eyes of God scatter all Evil

> *"A king who sits on the Throne of judgement scatters all evil with his eyes"*
>
> ### Proverbs 20:8

The light of the countenance of the 7 eyes of the Lord is powerful it goes to the depth of the heart to destroy darkness in the secret places, the light of the 7 eyes of God will exposes every forms of darkness inside the grave and in high places.

When the light of the countenance of the seven eyes of God shine forth upon the heart and the Spirit man of Saul that was converted and became Paul, on his way to Damascus as a former terrible persecutor of believers in Christ Jesus, suddenly the light struck him down and he was convicted of his sins and was convinced of the saving grace and the power of salvation through Jesus Christ the Lord of Lords.

"As he journeyed he came near Damascus and suddenly a light shone around him from heaven. Then he fell to the ground, and heard a voice saying to him, Saul, Saul, why are you persecuting Me?"

Acts 9: 3-4

"And he said, "Who are You, Lord? Then the Lord said, "I am JESUS, whom you are persecuting. It is hard for you to kick against the goads. So he, trembling and astonished, said, Lord, what do You want me to do? Then the Lord said to him, arise and go to into the city, and you will be told what you must do".

Acts 9: 5-6

The light of the countenance of the 7 eyes of God gives a clear understanding when it shines upon the eyes of your heart.

Strategic prayer counsel

1) Lord, give me clear vision. Enlighten my eyes of understanding.

2) Lord, let the light of the countenance of your 7 eyes shine upon the eyes of my Spirit man to understand what is in Your heart.

3) Lord, tune my spiritual antennae to recognise Your voice and be able to pick up quick messages from you and operate in the same frequency as You.

4) Lord, remove the dullness and darkness from my spiritual sight.

5) Lord, remove the planks and splinters from my eyes! Anything that causes our prophetic eyes to be blurred because of the fog of the world and the deceitfulness of sin, must be cleared in Jesus' name.

6) Lord, purge the eyes of my heart so that l can properly rule in the new Kingdom order and be properly positioned to do your will and impact my generation positively in Jesus' name.

"I pray that the eyes of your heart may be enlightened in order that you may know the hope to which He has called you, the riches of His glorious inheritance in His holy people."

Ephesians 1:18

As we see clearly we will move with authority, confidence and power and dominate our Kingdom inheritance to the glory of God's name.

NOTES

....
....
....
....
....
....
....
....
....
....
....
....
....
....
....
....
....
....

Chapter Five

The Spirit of the Godhead

"For in Him dwell all the fullness of the Godhead bodily; and you are complete in Him, who is the head of all principalities and power.

"In Him you were also circumcised with the circumcision made without hands, by putting off the body of the sins of the flesh, by the circumcision of Christ."

Colossians 2:9-11

The spirit of the Godhead is the fullness of the holy trinity – God the Father, Son and the Holy Spirit. The Holy Spirit is a person, a divine personality who has distinct personality traits. He is God living inside of all who have accepted Jesus Christ as their personal Lord and Saviour. He relates with us as a person whom we cannot see physically but is living inside of us. He is always present with us and can only take His leave or stand aside when we grieve Him and renounce Him.

The Holy Spirit is the executor of the Kingdom of God on earth. He is the revealer of the mysteries of the kingdom of God.

*"So Jesus said to them again, peace to you! As the
Father has sent Me, I also send you. And when He had
said this, He breathed on them, and said to them,
receive the Holy Spirit."*

John 20:21-22

Baptism with the Holy Spirit is imperative for all believers in
Christ Jesus who want to fulfill their Kingdom destiny, finish
well and be among the overcomers at the end of their earthly
journey.

Baptism with the Holy Spirit is the beginning of living a
supernatural life. Being baptised with the Holy Spirit is beyond
having sensational feelings and speaking in tongues, which
forms part of the manifestation and evidence that you have
been baptised with the Holy Spirit. When you are baptised
with the fullness of the Holy Spirit, you have a supernatural
experience that changes your life forever and makes you do
extraordinary things for God like the apostles did.

*"And it happened while Apollos was at Corinth, that
Paul, having passed through the upper regions, came
to Ephesus, And finding some disciples he said to them,
"Did you receive the Holy Spirit when you believed? So
they said to him, We have not so much as heard
whether there is a Holy Spirit. And he said unto them,
into what then were you baptized? So they said into*

John's baptism. Then Paul said John indeed baptized with a baptism of repentance, saying to the people that they should believe on Him who would come after him that is on Christ Jesus." When they heard this they were baptized in the name of the Lord Jesus."

Acts 19:1-5

"When Paul had laid hands on them, the Holy Spirit came upon them, and they spoke with tongues and prophesied."

Acts 19:6

Today, many Christians are ignorant of the existence and indispensability of the power of the Holy Spirit – even after repenting of their sins and being born again, they still don't receive the baptism of the Holy Spirit. It's no wonder sinners are comfortable in churches where they cannot feel the fire of the Holy Spirit and the worship and praise in the churches are not inspiring but entertaining! No wonder there is no more passion for souls that are perishing. Evangelism has become a thing of the past in our churches!

The extraordinary works of the apostles and their manifestations of supernatural power recorded in the Acts of the Apostles, occurred following the experience they had on the Day of Pentecost. After that day, they went forth and preached the gospel of the Kingdom everywhere, the Lord working with them and confirming the word with signs and wonders following, as recorded in Mark 16:20

They went beyond speaking in tongues, which was the initial evidence that they had been baptised with the Holy Spirit, to a life of extraordinary exploits and manifestation of the glory of God among the nations.

We need the fullness of the Holy Spirit in our daily lives. We need the fullness of the Holy Spirit always! When we are baptised with the fullness of the Holy Spirit, we will not be full of ourselves and Satan. There is no vacuum in the spirit realm. If you are not full of the Holy Spirit, you will be full of other contrary spirits. If you are not full of light, you will be vulnerable to the darkness!

It is the work of the Holy Spirit to get the secrets of the Kingdom of God and reveal them to us, He is the spirit of truth.

A Christian who is filled with the Holy Spirit lives victoriously irrespective of prevailing circumstances around him, and is effective in soul winning and subduing the kingdom of darkness. The salvation of souls is a supernatural work only made possible by the Holy Spirit's power. The Holy Spirit works in the lives of genuine Christians who have been baptised with the fullness of the Holy Spirit, to bring them into the fullness and image of Christ Jesus. He equips and brings Christian to perfection.

The Holy Spirit is our helper

> "And I will pray the Father, and He will give you another Helper, that He may abide with you forever. The Spirit of truth, whom the world cannot receive, because it neither sees Him nor knows Him; but you know Him, for He dwells with you and will be in you".
>
> ### John 14:16-17

> "But the Helper, the Holy spirit, who the Father will send in My name, He will teach you all things, and bring to your remembrance all things that I said to you."
>
> ### John 14:26

Our Lord and Saviour Jesus Christ promised that the Father will send the Holy Spirit after Jesus had ascended to the right hand of the Father in heaven. He was in a way promising to continue being present with believers in the person of the Holy Spirit, who would teach us all things.

With this knowledge at the back of his mind, Apostle Paul reiterated that the wisdom of the Holy Spirit is far greater than the wisdom of even the wisest in this world. The wisdom of the Holy Spirit is necessary to understand the gifts given to us freely by God. Indeed, we need the Holy Spirit to interpret spiritual truths so that, as disciples of the Lord Jesus, we can walk in truth. We need the Holy Spirit because God has chosen to reveal his mysteries to us and help us in our walk with Him through the power of the Holy Spirit.

The Holy Spirit is indeed everything we need. He is our all-in-all. He is the most important personality in our lives on earth. He gives us boldness to use our delegated authority that was purchased for us through the sacrifice of the blood of Jesus. The Holy Spirit is actually our Kingdom authority who empowers us with supernatural boldness to exercise our Kingdom mandate: to rule, reign, subdue and dominate the earth to the glory of His name. The Holy Spirit is given to us so that we can grow in grace and holiness in Christ Jesus and He guides us in our daily journey to eternity.

The Holy Spirit is the spirit of truth

As believers in Christ Jesus, we need to understand the love of God the Father as well as the work of the Holy Spirit in order to abide in God's word and become true disciples of Jesus Christ, striving to conform to His image and likeness. Through the unfailing love of God, the Holy Spirit allows you to be freed of your sins and iniquities and repent instead of being judged. He gives ability to believers to discern and have foresight of future events, He is the spirit of fire and truth, and He purifies by His fire and guides you into all truth.

"Nevertheless I tell you the truth. It is to your advantage that I go away; for if I do not go away, the Helper will not come to you; but if I depart, I will send Him to you. And when He has come, He will convict the world of sin, and of righteousness, and of judgment; of sin, because I go to My Father and you see Me no more."

John 16:7-10

The Holy Spirit is our guide

Jesus Christ declared that when the Holy Spirit comes, the spirit of truth, He will guide you into all truth. The Holy Spirit is the spirit of revelation. One acquires knowledge and skills from college, but the Holy Spirit gives progressive revelation, which is an application of knowledge.

"However, when He, the Spirit of truth, has come, He will guide you into all truth; for He will not speak on His own authority, but whatever He hears He will speak; and He will tell you things to come. He will glorify Me, for He will take of what is Mine and declare it to you.

John16:13-14

The Holy Spirit leads and gives direction at every point of decision in our lives. He glorifies God in us. He empowers us for service and guides us into all truth. He reveals unto us the understanding of our Kingdom inheritance and delivers us from great deception in these last days. The global reawakening that is coming will be championed by the world changers who will be empowered by the fullness of the Holy Spirit.

When my elder brother died in the hospital in 1989, I was not aware he was ill or that he was in hospital, but as l heard the Holy Spirit audibly, He spoke to me twice and said: "Where is your brother?" I replied that my brother would be at the church because he was the Sunday School Superintendent at his church. As l was exhausted after 72 hours of prophetic intercessory prayers with all the young women and men that l was training and mentoring at that time in Lagos, Nigeria, I discovered that l couldn't sleep until l inquired about the whereabouts of my brother from the Holy Spirit. l then heard Him say clearly that my brother was at Eko Hospital, and I was shocked knowing fully that the Holy Spirit would not lie.

When l arrived at Eko hospital, l saw his car parked outside the hospital and l went in straight to the nurses to inquire about him and l was told he was in the male medical ward. When l got to the male medical ward, behold l met my brother in deep pain and agony, and he said to me: "Janet, l have to die. l have concluded last night and repented of all my sins and I am sure I would see Jesus and will surely not miss heaven. Tell our parents not to weep and go to my office. Inside the drawer, you will see my bank account book You can take care of the money in my account..." As he was talking, he suddenly passed away and that would be the first time l ever saw a man die.

I quickly raised an altar right there and l told him: "Brother, you cannot die because l refuse to take a dead body from this hospital." I continued the intercession with a very strong reason why he must not die. For more than twenty minutes, l was interceding with tears rolling from my eyes. When l got to the point of bringing to God's remembrance the covenant relationship my brother had with Him and how l have witnessed his faithful service unto God and that he has not finished his purpose on earth. I said that if he died with an unfulfilled purpose, l would believe there is no God. At that point l heard an audible instruction again from the Holy Spirit. He said to me: "Cast out the spirit of death", which I did immediately.

The moment l obeyed the first instruction promptly, the Holy Spirit gave me further instructions and as I carried them out, my brother came back to life. The doctors were shocked because they had already given up on him the previous night before the Holy Spirit instructed me to go to the hospital. What amazed me was that he was discharged immediately without further treatment.

To this day, my brother has been a full time minister of the gospel of the Kingdom. Read the full story of this uncommon miracle in the book titled: *"My Death Experience: How Prayer Brought Me Back to Life."*

I learned from that day onwards that the Holy Spirit is the power that works inside of us and He will never leave us. When we obey His instructions promptly, He guides us into all truth and greater intimacy with Him, but when we disobey His prompts instructions, He will keep quiet and step aside. This is the reason why most believers in Christ Jesus do not hear the voice of the Holy Spirit often times.

The Holy Spirit is our transformer

> *"It is the Spirit who gives life; the flesh profits nothing..."*
>
> ### John 6:63

Only those who are filled with the Holy Spirit can transform the world that is covered in thick darkness. The release of the wave of the Holy Spirit will bring global revival to the churches, families and the nations. When our worship is filled with the Holy Spirit, there will be revival and the supernatural manifestation of His glory and power. The Holy Spirit will convict and reproof the world of sin. He will bring great help to us and relieve our infirmities and weaknesses.

"Now we have received, not the spirit of the world, but the Spirit who is from God, that we might know the things that have been freely given to us by God."

1 Corinthians 2:12

The Holy Spirit is our great intercessor

The Holy Spirit is our great intercessor because He actually knows what is in the mind of the Father. He helps believers in Christ Jesus to pray according to the will of God based on what is burning in the heart of God. The Holy Spirit understands the times and the seasons of our lives, and this is why He helps us to pray in line with what is in God's heart for us at every season of our lives on earth.

The most effective prayer is the prayer we pray by the counsel we receive from the Holy Spirit, the wisest counselor. When we learn to pray often in tongues, the Holy Spirit is very active in us and He reveals what is in the mind of God directly to us.

"Likewise the Spirit also helps in our weaknesses. For we do not know what we should pray for as we ought, but the Spirit Himself makes intercession for us with groaning which cannot be uttered. Now, He who searches the hearts knows what the mind of the Spirit

is, because He makes intercession for the saints according to the will of God"

Romans: 8:26-27.

We can only know the will of God through the help of the Holy Spirit. If you are praying about a particular burden or praying for somebody, mention the name of the person and begin to pray in tongues for a while and listen to the Holy Spirit.

I pray for my children by their names. After mentioning the name, I will speak in tongues for a while and the Holy Spirit will download to me what exactly my children are going through in their private lives and when l tell them whatever the Holy Spirit has revealed to me, they always ask me how l knew. I use this practical experience to teach them the importance of their intimacy with the Holy Spirit, which is really helping them in their Christian life journey.

The Holy Spirit is a great influencer

The Holy Spirit is an influencer who influences believers in Christ Jesus to do the will of God. When the Holy Spirit departs from you here on earth, you are like a dead person while you are still living. No wonder David prayed passionately in the book of Psalms.

"Create in me a clean heart, O God, and renew a steadfast Spirit within me. Do not cast me away from Your presence, And do not take Your Holy Spirit from me."

Psalm 51:10-11

The Holy Spirit influenced the conception and birth of the Lord Jesus Christ. He influenced the resurrection of the Lord Jesus. He announced the coming and second coming of the Lord Jesus. He influenced the creation of the heaven and the earth.

"In the beginning God created the heavens and the earth. The earth was without form, and void; and darkness was on the face of the deep. And the Spirit of God was hovering over the face of the waters. Then God said, let there be light, and there was light."

Genesis 1:1-3

The Holy Spirit influenced the temptation of Jesus in the wilderness. After Jesus fasted for forty days and forty nights and was hungry, He was led into the wilderness to be tempted by the devil right after His baptism by John. This reminds us that part of the preparation of Jesus for ministry came from a wilderness experience.

A wilderness experience is quite expedient for believers in Christ Jesus as priests of God to get our motives purified, our backbones solidified and our callings clarified. A wilderness experience is a screening process to measure our faith and identity in the sovereignty of God Almighty.

> *"Then Jesus was led up by the spirit into the wilderness to be tempted by the devil. And when He had fasted forty days and forty nights, afterward He was hungry. Now when the tempter came to Him, he said, "If you are the Son of God, command that these stones become bread. But He answered and said, It is written, Man shall not live by bread alone, but by every word that proceeds from the mouth of God."*

Matthew 4:1-4

In his book, *In the name of Jesus*, Henry Nouwen reminds us that the three temptations of Jesus correspond to three temptations believers face in their daily life journey.

- The temptation to be self-sufficient instead of complete trust in God in all things. Jesus trusted in God even with His legitimate needs.
- The temptation to gain publicity. Jesus refused to showcase His power to become a celebrity.
- The temptation to take shortcut to gain more power and fame for people to begin to worship Him.

The Holy Spirit influenced the three temptations and finally the temptation of Satan wanting Jesus to ascribe glory to

Himself instead of the heavenly Father that sent Him. After Jesus defeated the devil, the angels came and strengthened Him and ministered to Him.

The Holy Spirit influenced the resurrection of Jesus and His ascension into heaven; after He led captivity captive, He gave gifts unto men to fulfil the Father's promise. The Holy Spirit influences the use of our spiritual gifts with signs and wonders to the glory of God.

> *"And it shall come to pass in the last days, says God, That I will pour out of My Spirit on all flesh; Your sons and your daughters shall prophesy, Your young men shall see visions, Your old men shall dream dreams. And on My menservants and on My maidservants I will pour out My spirit in those days; And they shall prophesy, I will show wonders in heaven above and signs in the earth beneath; Blood and fire and vapor of smoke."*

Acts 2:17-18

The Holy Spirit influences radical evangelism with boldness. This was displayed in the lives of Peter and John. After they were baptised with the Holy Spirit, they taught the people and healed a lame man who was lame from his mother's womb. This miracle was influenced by the power of the Holy Spirit. After this miracle, many people believed Peter and John's gospel of repentance and believed in Jesus Christ of Nazareth. Peter spoke and preached the gospel with boldness by the power of the Holy Spirit.

> *"Then Peter filled with the Holy spirit, said to them, "Rulers of the people and elders of Israel; If we this day are judged for good deed done to a helpless man, by what means he has been made well, let it be known to you all, and to all the people of Israel, that by the name of Jesus Christ of Nazareth, whom you crucified, whom God raised from the dead, by Him this man stands here before you whole. This is the stone which was rejected by you builders, which has become the chief cornerstone. Nor is there salvation in any other, for there is no other name under heaven given among men by which we must be saved."*
>
> ### Acts 4:8-12

The Holy Spirit sanctifies us

The word sanctification means "made holy, consecrated, being set apart for special use". The Holy Spirit works in us to sanctify us, consecrate us and makes us holy because He is holy and He cannot dwell in an unholy vessel.

"That I might be a minister of Jesus Christ to the Gentiles, ministering the gospel of God that the offering of the Gentiles might be acceptable, sanctified by the Holy Spirit."

Romans 15:16

When the Holy Spirit is fully present in us, it is very difficult for sin to be present because He brings an atmosphere of holiness with Him. If we continue in sin, our flesh has to literally resist the Holy Spirit. When Isaiah encountered the Holy Spirit, he suddenly became aware of his own frailty and needed sanctification. The angel had to place a coal on his lips to sanctify him in Isaiah 6:1-7.

Jesus Christ was filled with both anointing and the Holy Spirit. It is not enough to have the anointing without sanctification, thus only manifesting the gifts of the Holy Spirit which is without repentance; even though God will not take the gifts from you or hinder you from using the gifts. It's no wonder that some ministers experience the anointing, yet sin is rampant in their lives. The anointing comes strictly for ministering to someone else, while the Holy Spirit comes to change us inside and out.

I will never forget the day l was converted by the Holy Spirit — 27ᵗʰ April 1985. Two sisters were having a night prayer and l came to the sister that owned the apartment, being my boyfriend's sister. l was there to write the University's admission examination in the city where the sister lived. I was studying in the living room and at around 22:00, the other sister joined her and they urged me to go into the room and continue my studies so that I would not be disturbed. I resisted their advice and told them that l would be fine and that they should continue with their prayers.

They started with worship and later started speaking in tongues continuously. At a point, the Holy Spirit caught up with me and l started weeping profusely with deep pain in my heart over all the sins that l have ever committed. Without anyone preaching to me, l started confessing my sins one after the other with tears, crying for forgiveness and mercy. I wept for almost ten minutes in deep pain as l remembered all the sins l had committed. I realised that l had been in rebellion against Jesus, who had died for me.

After l stopped weeping and confessing my sins, the two sisters led me to Christ Jesus and prayed for me and assured me that l was then born again and that my name had been written in the book of life. It is amazing that from that point, l couldn't do all that l used to have pleasure in doing to please myself. l surrendered my will to Jesus and always wanting to do His pleasure. The Holy Spirit is the greatest evangelist that converts and reconciles us back to God, our heavenly Father.

The Holy Spirit sanctifies by washing the heart and renewing the mind. He assures us of the indwelling presence of Jesus Christ, helping us understand the word of God, building our faith, and showing us our heavenly Kingdom inheritance after we make the decision to live in the spirit and not in the flesh.

The Holy Spirit bears witness

The Holy Spirit is the personality living inside of us, bearing witness and strengthening our faith. The Spirit Himself bears witness with our spirit that we are children of God.

> *"For as many as are led by the Spirit of God, these are sons of God. For you did not receive the spirit of bondage again to fear, but you received the Spirit of adoption by whom we cry out, Abba Father. The Spirit Himself bears witness with our Spirit that we are children of God."*
>
> ### Romans 8:14-16

The Holy Spirit protects us from falling by witnessing to our spirit when we are going astray, He will never condone sin or any form of unrighteousness because He is holy.

The Holy Spirit enables us to evangelise

The Holy Spirit gives us boldness to do the work of an evangelist, witnessing to unbelievers and preaching the gospel of the Kingdom to them that are lost and perishing.

We cannot be too full of the Holy Spirit, therefore it is imperative that we ask God for the fullness of the Holy Spirit daily. The Holy Spirit desires that we communicate with Him most often and ask Him for direction and counsel before we make decisions.

He wants us to engage Him in worship very often; when we worship in the spirit and sing in tongues, He reveals deep things from God unto us because He knows what is in the heart of God. When we pray in tongues more than in our own understanding, we have deeper revelation about the mind of God; we cannot get to the deepest part of His thoughts without the Holy Spirit.

The Holy Spirit help us to hear God's Voice

> "My SHEEP hear My voice, and I know them, and they follow Me. And I give them eternal life, and they shall never perish; neither shall anyone snatch them out of My hand."
>
> **John 10:27**

God created the earth through the spoken word. He also sent Jesus, His only begotten Son as the word that lived among us. God still speaks to those who believe in Him and accept Jesus as their personal Lord and Saviour.

As believers in Christ Jesus, it is imperative to discover and understand how God speaks and relates to you. Hearing God's voice requires you to train your spiritual senses and be filled with the Holy Spirit. You need to be familiar with the language of the Holy Spirit and have an intimate relationship with the Holy Spirit and often living in God's presence.

When you give your life to Jesus Christ, you have entered into a Covenant relationship with God.

Part of the Terms and condition of the covenant relationship is baptism of the HOLY SPIRIT. If you are born again and you are not yet baptized with the Holy Spirit with the evidence of speaking in Tongues, you are not complete and you are still joking! You are still a Church goer NOT a Kingdom believer!

HOLY SPIRIT is the seal of our Covenant relationship with God that is our salvation. He is the Voice of God to us.

If you have not discovered how to hear God's voice clearly as kingdom believer, your spiritual growth will be stagnant!

You will not be able to understand your Kingdom Identity, you will fall for less!

You will not be able to fulfil your kingdom destiny and finish well!

You will not be able to have a deep relationship with God!

You will not be able to choose the right career and profession in life.

You must not go into marriage covenant relationship if you are not sure of hearing God's voice clearly.

You will never be able to know the sovereign will of God in marriage if you don't know how God speaks to you.

You must not go into Ministry if you don't know how God speaks to you.

You cannot engage in spiritual warfare if you don't know how God speaks.

Hearing God's voice is part of our Kingdom benefits that will be added unto us after seeking first the Kingdom of God and His righteousness. Matthew 6:33

Hearing God's voice is imperative as a Priest and King. Revelation 5:10

All Kingdom believer is a King and Priest who must reign on Earth!

Hearing God Speaks at 3 Levels

1) Hearing through vision – Open vision, Vision of the night (Dream) and supernatural vision of angels and Supernatural being.
2) Physical hearing – Audible voices and Still small voices.
3) The word of God – Through Prophets and apostles.

DREAM is not an authentic way of confirming the voice of God! Satan also use dream to confuse and contaminate your vision! Your dream must have a back-up of clear word of God, through discerning of spirit and intuitive understanding of God's word. 1 Samuel 3:1-22.

The process of hearing God's Voice

Samuel learned to live in God's presence, he learned to listen and respond to God. As a consecrated reigning priest, Samuel was always properly dressed with his consecrated priestly attire – a linen ephod which symbolised purity inside and outside – with the fullness of the Holy Spirit. He separated himself from all the appearances of darkness that cover the earth; he circumcised his heart with all diligence and did not allow his *garments and priesthood* to be **polluted and defiled!**

He consecrated his ears, not having itching ears that listen to gossip and unproductive conversation that impair the ears from hearing God's Voice clearly. Samuel understood that he was into a covenant relationship with God and he determined to be a useful vessel in God's hand and a blessing to his generation.

Samuel grew up under Eli's tutelage, but God bypassed Eli and started speaking to Samuel after Eli lost his credibility before God. Eli lost his kingdom focus; he blinded himself to his error, failure, assumptions and presumptuous sins.

Although Eli was always present in God's tabernacle, he was always distracted and full of unproductive activities. Suddenly there was a paradigm shift in his motives, thoughts, imagination, attitude, devotion, preferences and perspectives to life and the word of God.

Eli could no longer discern, see clearly and hear God's voice for his generational redemptive purpose. No wonder Eli turned to folly with secret faults and presumptuous sins with his two sons. Eli could no longer see and discern the abomination that was standing right in the holy tabernacle of God. What is a priest doing in God's tabernacle if he can no longer hear the voice of God clearly?

To this day God is still busy revealing deep secrets to those who fear Him and dwell in His awesome presence in this deceptive world and particularly in this defining season. We must listen to His voice carefully.

Hindrances to Hearing God's Voice

1) Faulty spiritual foundation (Being a Church goer not Kingdom believer)
2) Faulty ancestral foundation (Dual ancestral priesthood impair the ears)

3) Uncircumcised HEART (Polluted and impure Heart) Idolatry in your Heart
4) Lack of knowledge of the Word of God
5) Legitimate and illegitimate distractions (Busyness of this world)
6) Secret fault and presumptuous sins
7) Lack of Mentorship
8) Lack of knowledge of your kingdom Identity.
9) Lack of Vision
10) Religious tradition and wrong mindset

Strategic prayers

- Lord, show me your mercy and cleanse me from all secret faults that may prevent me from hearing you clearly.

- Lord, keep me back from presumptuous sins that may block my spiritual inner ears from hearing your voice.

- Lord, deliver me from a flat nose and marred vision that cannot discern and let your fire consume every defect in my eyes that l may see clear visions.

- Lord, deliver my mind from distractions while l am in your presence that l may be focused and hear you clearly by the power of the HOLY SPIRIT.

"but whoever listens to Me will live in safety and be at ease, without fear or harm."

Proverbs 1:33 (NIV)

Presently, lots of distractions, deception, idolatry and noises are preventing us from listening, hearing and responding to God's voice. Yet the heavens are declaring the glory of God daily, day unto day uttered speech and night unto night reveals His deep knowledge!

Consecration involves revelation about the state of our heart, our motives, thoughts, objectives and intentions in life. True revelation about yourself is all about your HEART.

Who you are in the sight of God is the reflection about your HEART, which is more important to God than what we do for God! When Isaiah's heart and tongue were cleansed, his pattern of vision and revelation changed! (Isaiah 6:1)

Operational strategies for hearing God's voice

- Circumcise and consecrate your heart with all diligence (Proverbs 4:23).

- Genuine salvation with the fullness of the HOLY SPIRIT (Be sure that the kingdom of God is established in your heart. Don't just be a church goer)

- Be delivered from all ancestral faulty foundation

- Be ready to pay the sacrifice, seeking the Lord personally most often
- Understand your kingdom purpose/ destiny on the earth.
- Be hungry for the word of the Lord
- Study the word of God most often, for God speaks through His word.

Pragmatic strategies for hearing God's voice

- Raise a new and true altar to God with a heart of gratitude and consistent worship (Genesis 12:7-8).
- Forgive easily and let go as you go to God's presence.
- Avoid evil jealousy and competition; you are unique in your calling and purpose. Cast down all arguments and every high thing that exalts itself against the knowledge of God from your heart (2 Corinthians 10:5).
- Bring every evil thought and imagination into captivity to the obedience of Christ.
- Avoid thoughts of bitterness and resentment.
- Do not occupy your heart with unnecessary worries, frivolities and comments that are irrelevant to your Kingdom purpose.

- Avoid unproductive conversations, gossip, backstabbing and unnecessary jesting. It impairs the ears!

- Short the gate of your heart against every forms of distractions when you are praying.

- Pray in tongue and worship more in the Spirit for at least 30 minutes daily.

- Engage in Listening Prayers after praying in tongues....Listen for 2-3minutes. Pay attention to the Holy Spirit's prompting in your heart.

- Tell God that you love Him and acknowledge His sovereignty over your life.

- Focus the lens of your heart to God at the throne of grace.

- Sometimes, God will start speaking to you with the word "I LOVE YOU and I CARE FOR YOU".

- Sometimes it may be a verse of the scripture that will come to your heart and when you read it, it will be accurate for your situation.

Do not grieve the Holy Spirit

The Holy Spirit will step aside when you engage in sinful acts and disobedience to His instructions. In order not to grieve the Holy Spirit, you must walk in the Spirit so you do not fulfill the lust of the flesh. Any foul language and blasphemy against the Holy Spirit cannot be forgiven because He is God living inside of us.

> *"Assuredly, I say to you, all sins will be forgiven the sons of men, and whatever blasphemies they may utter, but he who blasphemes against the Holy Spirit never has forgiveness, but is subject to eternal condemnation. Because they said He has an unclean spirit."*
>
> ### Mark 3:28-29

Therefore I say to you, every sin and blasphemy will be forgiven men, but the blasphemy against the Holy Spirit will not be forgiven men."

This is very crucial for us as believers in Christ Jesus to be careful not to grieve the Holy Spirit and blaspheme against Him. This is the only and one unpardonable sin in the Bible!" Matthew 12:31-32

> *"And do not grieve the Holy spirit of God, by whom you were sealed for the day of Redemption, Let all bitterness, wrath, anger, clamor, and evil speaking be put away from you, with all malice. And be kind to one another, tenderhearted, forgiving one another, even as God in Christ forgave you."*
>
> ### Ephesians 5:30-32

After meditating on this unpardonable sin, blasphemy against the Holy Spirit, the insight l got is that the Holy Spirit is God inside of us, living in us, giving us the breath of life. When you use abusive language and blaspheme against the Holy Spirit, you are actually speaking against God. No wonder that no one from the foundation of the earth who has ever blasphemed or boasted against God will live to see the light of the next day! Remember the Titanic that sank and many more uncountable examples.

The important lesson here for us as overcomers in Christ Jesus is to be careful not to grieve the Holy Spirit and make the Holy Spirit sad through the words of our mouth and our actions.

Our Words

We should avoid:

- Abusive language;
- Obscene and foul language;
- Profanity; and
- Corrupt and evil words

Our Actions

- Bitterness makes the Holy Spirit sorrowful.

- Bitterness is an embittered and resentful spirit that refuses to be reconciled.

- Bitter people spread bitterness and malice according to Hebrews 12:15.

- Uncontrolled anger must be addressed.

- Unforgiveness grieves the Holy Spirit according to Ephesians 4:29

If a believer keeps grieving the Holy Spirit with these actions, words and weakness of character, it makes you vulnerable to attacks from the devil who has come to kill, steal and destroy. It also blocks the spiritual realm around you and hinders your prayers.

May the Lord help us and enlighten our eyes of understanding so we do not fall into the last days' snares and the deceitfulness of sins, in Jesus' powerful name. Amen.

NOTES

....
....
....
....
....
....
....
....
....
....
....
....
....
....
....
....
....
....

Chapter Six
The Spirit of Wisdom

Spiritual Wisdom

However, we speak wisdom among those who are mature, yet not the wisdom of this age, nor of the rulers of this age, who are coming to nothing. But we speak the wisdom of God in a mystery, the hidden wisdom which God ordained before the ages for our glory. Which none of the rulers of this age knew; for had they known, they would not have crucified the Lord of glory.

> "But as it is written; Eye has not seen, nor ear heard, nor have entered into the heart of man the things which God has prepared for those who love Him.

> "But God has revealed them to us through His Spirit. For the Spirit searches all things, yes the deep things of God. For what man knows the things of a man except the spirit of the man which is in him? Even so no one knows the things of God except the Spirit of God.

> "Now we have received, not the Spirit of the world, but the Spirit who is from God, that we might know the things that have been freely given to us by God.

"These things we also speak, not in words which man's wisdom teaches but which the Holy Spirit teaches, comparing spiritual thins with spiritual.

"But the natural man does not receive the things of the Spirit of God, for they are foolishness to him; nor can he know them, because they are spiritually discerned."

1 Corinthians 2:6-14

The contemporary meaning of wisdom is the ability to know what is true or right, common sense or the collection of one's knowledge. The spirit of wisdom is the divine grace given by the Lord to apply knowledge and implement the right counsel among men on the earth. The benefits of walking in His wisdom are great. The first blessing is greater knowledge of God. The lord is personally involved in every facet of our lives. The better we know His character, the more we will understand His viewpoints, recognise where He is working, and be able to respond properly to life's circumstances and challenges.

A second way we profit is by receiving clear guidance. God sees everything – His perspective is eternal, and every decision He makes is perfect. He knows exactly what is necessary to accomplish His will in our lives, and what it will take to resolve problems in a Godly way, making us more like Christ.

A third benefit is divine protection. As Proverbs 28:26 tells us, He who trusts in his own heart is a fool, but whomever walks wisely will be delivered. We are not to rely upon our emotions, which are easily influenced by ungodliness. Nor can we trust the world's opinions.

The baptism of the spirit of wisdom brings divine protection and discerning of spirits. You will be able to discern the intent of the heart of man and be able to make wise decisions on what steps to take at every point in life. The spirit of wisdom enables us to gain insight into the unseen and the unspoken because nothing is hidden from the Spirit of God.

The baptism of the spirit of wisdom enables you to get to know God intimately and have clear guidance and direction, which human wisdom cannot provide. This only comes from the Heavenly Father.

"Wisdom is the principal thing; therefore get wisdom:
and with all thy getting get understanding"
Proverbs 4:7.

According to David Chan "Wisdom refers to the ability to see the 'big picture' and translate one's experience and knowledge into good judgement and decisions," adding that it is less about academic intelligence. Wisdom is one of such things which are indispensable in having a fulfilled and successful life. In other words, wisdom is an acquisition we cannot do without in life.

That is why the Bible is so emphatic about the importance of wisdom. The Bible says in Proverbs 3:13, "Happy is the man that findeth wisdom, and the man that getteth understanding.

As Michael Bradley insists in his article, "All Knowledge and Wisdom comes direct from God," all the "treasures" of wisdom and knowledge are "hidden" in God the Father and Jesus Christ. With such wisdom, you can overcome every problem or crisis in your life, because wisdom will always make you think before talking or acting. Therefore, in your spiritual, academic and social life, always seek godly wisdom from the Lord, because the wisdom of the world is for the world only.

Godly wisdom is the ability and grace to understand God's perspective on situations and respond accordingly. It brings us the strength to stand firm in our faith and choose His way. It also helps us to calmly accept the hardships in our lives. Our sovereign God knows the extent of our difficulties. Out of His love for us, He never gives us more than we can handle.

God wants to prosper His people in spiritual as well as material ways. For that reason, His first priority is to increase our understanding of Him. Then, as we align our hearts with His wisdom and will, we can apply His principles not just to our finances but to every facet of life. The Lord stands ready to pour out His choicest blessings, power, divine favour, spiritual prosperity, and supernatural peace on those who draw near to Him and submit to His will.

The spirit of wisdom equips us for position, teaches and reveals God's judgement and justice and how to exercise it. It teaches us how to be skillful and wise in our mind, words, and actions about the rules of rulership and releases contentment and joy that produces delight towards God's heart.

Presently the sons of God who have been set free by the blood of Jesus and given the grace to show forth and manifest God's glory to unlock the wealth of the nations, rule, reign, subdue the powers of darkness and dominate their kingdom inheritance with their delegated authority are still in bondage and slavery – confused, frustrated and deceived with unconscious ignorance and lack of knowledge and clear understanding.

Now is the season of restoration of God's seven Spirits with His glory and power, the season of sweeping away the counterfeit with the refuse of lies and manifesting the Glory of God!

God is a God of purpose and seasons. He operates through seasons and timing not by the earthly calendar which is January to December with days, hours, minutes and seconds. He operates with the heavenly hosts and relates with all what He has created through His own heavenly calendar, which is through seasons and times.

"To everything there is a season. A time for every purpose under heaven."

Ecclesiastes 3:1

God has created all things for His own pleasure and to manifest the Glory and power of God on planet earth. You and I are created for God's own pleasure! The moment our lives are not manifesting God's glory and we are not living for His pleasure, rather living for our own pleasure and the pleasure of our flesh and to glorify our fleshly desires and the devil, we are living a wasted and meaningless life. This is a tragedy!

The saints of God have the responsibility to choose to shine forth the light of God or be covered with darkness. There is no siting on the fence and there is no vacuum in the realm of the spirit.

Any Christian that refuses to cooperate with God and reveal His glory with the shining forth of the light of God in him-/herself will be covered in darkness. We have been created to have dominion in life over the principalities and powers that control darkness.

"The heavens declare the glory of God; And the firmament shows His handiwork, Day unto day utters speech, and night unto night reveals knowledge. There is no speech nor language where their voice is not heard"

Psalm 19:1-3

The Sun, Stars and the Moon show forth the wisdom and the glory of God in their seasons and time. The sun will never rise in the night while the moon will not rise during the day. The moon only rises at night, which is the time meant for the moon to show forth the glory of God and to manifest the power of God on earth for God's pleasure. Every tree that bears fruit is scheduled to bring forth its fruit in the appointed season. Trees bear their fruit in their different seasons to fulfill a particular purpose, which will give God pleasure and glorify His name in the life of His creation.

Oranges and lemons that contain vitamin C, which is necessary during winter season, are available in abundance and cheaper during winter, because that is the season the fruits are mostly needed and it comes forth more abundantly in its season to fulfil its ultimate purpose. This is the wisdom of God.

Faith is absolute confidence in God's wisdom, His power and His goodness. God gave stewardship to human beings over the works of His hands and have bestowed us with our gifts, talents, time, seasons, assets and relationships.

For we are His workmanship, created in Christ Jesus for good works, which God prepared beforehand that we should walk in them.

Ephesians 2:10

Stewardship means that we are going to be responsible to report on how we have managed God's given time, our gifts, potentials, assets, Kingdom resources and relationships to His glory.

We need the spirit of wisdom to manage and redeem our God's given time to us. We need the spirit of wisdom to manage our Kingdom identity. We need the spirit of wisdom to manage our gifts and talents and we need the spirit of wisdom to manage our relationships with God and with people here on earth.

The spirit of wisdom is a Godly attribute and a close relationship with God will impart you with wisdom.

> *"For the Lord giveth wisdom; out of His mouth cometh knowledge and understanding."*
> **Psalm 2:6**

The baptism of the spirit of wisdom imparts us with intuitive understanding of the mysteries of God and it produces deep revelation knowledge.

The seven pillars of wisdom

1) Wisdom is from God, He Himself is the one who grants enduring wisdom. The Lord by wisdom founded the earth; by understanding He established the heavens; by

His knowledge the depths were broken up, and clouds drop down the dew (Proverbs 3:19-20).

2) Wisdom adds value to your life. Wisdom is profitable to direct and wisdom brings great success (Ecclesiastes 10:10).

3) Wisdom is better than strength. Through wisdom a house is built, and by understanding it is established; by knowledge the rooms are filled with all precious and pleasant riches. It gives you unprecedented grace to triumph (Proverbs 24:3).

4) Wisdom will deliver you from many troubles. There is safety in wisdom. Wisdom enables you to have more understanding than your enemies. It delivers you from error and making numerous mistakes (Psalm 119:98).

5) Wisdom is a defense and it gives more life to those who have it abundantly. Wisdom is good with an inheritance, and profitable to those who see the sun, for wisdom is a defense as money is a defense, but the excellence of knowledge is that wisdom gives life to those who have it (Ecclesiastes 7:11-12).

6) Wisdom enables you to receive deep revelation and deep understanding of the knowledge of the sovereignty of God and the exceeding greatness of His power that works inside of you (Ephesians 1:17-18).

7) Wisdom enlightens your eyes of understanding to know the hope of your calling and get the enduring riches of the glory of His inheritance through Christ Jesus. Wisdom lets you stand strong with the understanding of your Kingdom identity and spiritual authority to fulfill your Kingdom destiny (Ephesians 1:18-19).

The Excellence of Wisdom ~ Proverbs 8:12-36

I wisdom, dwell with prudence, and find out knowledge and discretion. By me kings' reign, and rulers decree justice. By me princes rule, and nobles, all the judges of the earth. I love those who love me, and those who seek me diligently will find me.

Riches and honour are with me, Enduring riches and righteousness, My fruit is better than gold, yes, than fine gold, and my revenue than choice silver. I traverse the way of righteousness, in the midst of the paths of justice, that I may cause those who love me to inherit wealth, that I may fill their treasuries.

The Lord possessed me (Wisdom) at the beginning of His way, before His works of old. I have been established from everlasting, from the beginning, before there were heaven and earth. Before the mountains were settled, before the hills, I was brought forth. When He prepared the heavens, I was there, when He drew a circle on the face of the deep, when He assigned to the sea its limit, so that the waters would not transgress His command, when He marked out the foundations of the earth, then I was beside Him as a master craftsman, and I was daily His delight, rejoicing always before Him, rejoicing in His inhabited world, and my delight was with the sons of men.

Wisdom multiplies your life span. Whoever finds Wisdom finds life and obtains favour from the Lord.

The Spirit of wisdom creates

The Spirit of wisdom transforms

The Spirit of wisdom reveals the truth

The Spirit of wisdom liberates

The Spirit of wisdom equip and empower

The Spirit of wisdom establish the work of your hands with glory

The Spirit of wisdom releases commanded blessings abundantly.

Creative Wisdom

"The Lord by wisdom created the earth; by understanding He established the heavens; by His knowledge the depths were broken up, And clouds drop down the dew".

Proverbs 3:19

The Spirit of wisdom gives ability to create and re-create, wisdom gives you witty inventions and great ideas as part of God's nature and likeness in which we are created to do awesome things on the earth to the glory of God's name.

"He has made the earth by His power; He has established the world by His wisdom, and stretched out the heaven by His understanding".

Jeremiah 51:15

Protective Wisdom

The Spirit of wisdom gives life to your soul, it place on your head an ornament of grace and glory. It brings honour upon your life. Your steps will never be hindered when you walk in wisdom, when you run, you will not stumble with wisdom neither fall, and wisdom will preserve your life and protect you in time of trouble.

Strategic Prayers for Wisdom
1. Lord, baptize me with seven fold Spirit of wisdom and revelation knowledge to understand the riches of the glory of His inheritance in the saints.
2. Lord, baptize me with the seven fold Spirits of wisdom and knowledge to understand the exceeding greatness of your power which you work in Christ Jesus.
3. Lord baptize me with the 7 fold Spirit of knowledge and understanding to make know your manifold wisdom to the principalities and powers in the heavenly places.

Chapter Seven

The Spirit of Understanding

Understanding is the ability to comprehend something with insight or good judgement. To have an understanding of something is to have deep insight with good judgement on that particular subject. Understanding is clear comprehension of the information you receive from the true source. It also gives you the ability to intuitively understand enigmas, solve problems and comprehend things quickly.

> *"The entrance of your words gives light; it gives understanding to the simple."*
>
> **Psalm 119:13**

> *"And all the people went their way to eat and drink, to send portions and rejoice greatly, because they understood the words that were declared to them."*
>
> **Nehemiah 8:12**

After Ezra had read the word of God to the people and the Levites had explained it, they understood the words and went away with great rejoicing in their hearts. The spirit of understanding quickens the spirit man and activates the joy of the Lord in your heart. The joy of believers in Christ Jesus reflects the glory of God when you have the understanding of the true knowledge of the word of God and His sovereign identity.

When the Israelites had a deep understanding of the word of God, there was a paradigm shift in the way they worshipped God. They started worshipping with overflowing joy that flooded their hearts, because the heart of their understanding was opened by the light of the countenance of the seven Spirits of God.

This is why Paul prayed fervently for the saints in Ephesus that their heart of understanding would be enlightened, that they may know the hope of His calling, the riches of the glory of His inheritance in the saints, and the exceeding greatness of His power toward us who believe according to the working of His mighty power. This is the same power that worked in Christ Jesus when He raised Him from the dead and seated Him at His right hand in the heavenly places, far above all principalities and power and might and dominion.

The Lord baptised Solomon with the spirit of understanding and wisdom, which imparted him with the knowledge of wise counsel to discern the right justice to put all things in order, to order the Kingdom in a right way according to the sovereign will of God at the right time and fulfill His counsel in his appointed season.

"Now O Lord my God, You have made your servant king instead of my father David, but I am a little child, I do not know how to go out or come in. And your servant is in the midst of your people whom you have chosen a great people, too numerous to be numbered or counted.

"Therefore give to your servant an UNDERSTANDING HEART to judge your people that I may discern between good and evil, for who is able to judge this great people of yours".

1 Kings 3:7-8

The spirit of understanding enables you to discern and choose what is good and reject evil. Solomon was delivered from all the evil counselors that surrounded him because God gave him the spirit of wisdom and an understanding heart. This also enabled him to make accurate decisions at the right time.

The baptism of the spirit of understanding delivered Solomon from unnecessary stress and hardship. He could discern when to hide himself and rest before appearing to people. He rested before experiencing burnout. he was not always burnt out before he go to rest.

The Spirit of Understanding Preserves Life

The baptism of the Spirit of understanding delivered Solomon from unnecessary stress and hardship.

"Behold, I have done according to your words; see, I have given you a wise and understanding heart, so that there has not been any one like you before you, nor shall any like you arise after you. And I have also given you what you have not asked: both riches and honour, so that there shall not be anyone like you among the kings all your days."

1 Kings 3:12-13

The baptism of the Spirit of understanding gives you the discretion to understand time and season to do the right thing at the right time for the right reasons like the Sons of Issachar who understood the times and knew what Isreal ought to do at the right time.1 Chronicles 12:32.

The baptism of the spirit of wisdom and understanding brought Solomon to the place of prosperity and riches through covenant. Instead of asking for riches and prosperity, it is wise to first ask for the baptism of the spirit of understanding and wisdom. When you are baptised with the spirit of wisdom and understanding, doors of prosperity will open in the right direction at the right time without sorrow.

The baptism of the spirit of wisdom and understanding enabled Daniel to be wiser than the astrologers in his time. Daniel received deep insight to the dream of the king with accurate interpretation. The spirit of understanding gives ability to discern deep things in the heart of man and gives insights to the deep secrets in the heart of God.

> *"Daniel answered and said: Blessed is the name of God forever and ever, for wisdom and might is His. And He changes the times and the seasons; He removes kings and rises up kings; He gives wisdom to the wise and knowledge to those who have understanding.*
>
> *"He reveals deep and secret things; He knows what is in the darkness, and light dwells with him"*
>
> ### Daniel 2:20-22

Antidotes to access the Spirit of Understanding

The baptism of the spirit of understanding gives you deep insights to have an intuitive understanding of time and seasons like the sons of Issachar. The baptism of the spirit of understanding inspired Mordecai to motivate Esther to act at the right time.

> *"Then the kings said to the wise men who understood the times (for this was the king's manner toward all who knew law and justice...)"*
>
> ### Esther 1:13

Whole-hearted obedience unto God will unlock your understanding in the knowledge of God; obedience will reveal to you the secret things in the heart of God.

In order for someone to fulfill their Kingdom destiny on earth, it is imperative to be baptised with the spirit of understanding, as this enables you to understand your uniqueness, potential and Kingdom identity, and you will seek the Lord to have the understanding of the particular time and season to fulfill your Kingdom purpose and finish well. To every purpose on earth, there is a season of fulfillment.

Apostle Paul said, be prepared in season and out of season, he recognised that he was in the winter of his ministry, and therefore he poured his knowledge into his successor, Timothy.

Who are you pouring yourself into as your mentee to take the baton from you after your departure and carry the Kingdom legacy forward to the next generation?

The baptism of the spirit of understanding draws out counsel from the deepest part of the heart and enables you to know and understand the secret things in the heart of men and God and thereby be wiser than the enemies of God on the earth including principalities and powers in high places.

"Counsel in the heart of man is like deep water; but a man of understanding will draw it out"

Proverbs 20:5

NOTES

....
....
....
....
....
....
....
....
....
....
....
....
....
....
....
....
....
....

Chapter Eight
The Spirit of Knowledge

The spirit of knowledge is the spirit of discovery. Knowledge is the information you receive from the true source. Wisdom is application of knowledge, the act of putting into practice whatever knowledge you have received. What you know is the product of what you have learned.

Learning affects permanent change in behaviour after you have received information through teaching, studying, watching and revelation. The level of the revelation knowledge you have is what will make you live an abundant life and finish well. You cannot give what you don't know you have nor can you give what you don't have.

Knowledge is the key to freedom. The key to knowledge is truth. The greatest enemy of man is ignorance!

The knowledge of the truth is what sets you free. There are some theological errors, taught in the theology colleges that put people in spiritual bondage The Holy Spirit is the spirit of truth, the baptism of the fullness of the seven Spirits of God gives revelation knowledge of the truth.

"My people are destroyed for lack of knowledge; because thou hast rejected knowledge, I will also reject thee from being priest for Me; because you have forgotten the law of your God, I will also forget your children".

Hosea 4:6

Ignorance is a terrible spiritual disease. When you are battling with ignorance, you don't need any enemy to destroy your work and God's investment in your life, because you will destroy it yourself.

It does not even matter how hardworking a man may be, if he lacks knowledge and the correct application of his knowledge, he will be limited and find it difficult to shine forth his glory.

That's why Paul told the Romans that those who refused to receive and retain the knowledge of God, He gave over to a debased state of mind which made them do foolish things which are not fitting. Be careful not to waste God's investment in your life due to a lack of knowledge

"And even as they did not like to retain God in their knowledge. God gave them over to a debased mind, to do those things which are not fitting"

Romans 1:28

God is all-knowing. He has all the knowledge of heaven and earth and He expects us, whom He has created in His own image to act like Him and reason like Him. That is why He gave us the authority to rule, reign, subdue the kingdom of darkness and dominate the earth for His glory. He made us His legal representatives on earth and gave us the opportunity to be baptised with the spirit of the revelation knowledge, so that we can enforce His will on the earth as it is being done in heaven. We have His mandate and delegated authority and He is ever present with us, backing us up until the end of time.

Perception in the Spirit

The discipline of your spirit man will take you beyond the natural realm to the spirit realm where you perceive the light of God in the spirit and enlightenment through the word of God by the Holy Spirit that enables you to receive revelation knowledge.

The baptism of the spirit of knowledge gives you inner peace. You will not be moved by whatever you see, but you will be strong and confident in the knowledge of the word of God that is inside of you.

The Lord wants us to operate with the spirit of revelation knowledge. When you are baptised with the spirit of revelation knowledge, it enlightens your inner being and you receive progressive revelation knowledge of the secrets in the heart of God and discernment of the hearts of people.

The movement and awakening during this end times will come through the Spirit of revelation knowledge to kick-start the revival. Revelation knowledge heals your spiritual eyes to begin to see clearly and it brings enlightenment from God that brings new understanding and revelation into your spirit man.

- Revelation knowledge makes you excel in all things.
- Revelation knowledge dissolves doubts.
- Revelation knowledge brings transformation.
- Revelation knowledge restores peace.
- Revelation knowledge brings confidence.
- Revelation knowledge ignites and authenticates your authority.
- Revelation knowledge establishes and authenticates your priesthood.
- Revelation knowledge brings impartation.
- Revelation knowledge generates light and perfection.

"And you Daniel, shut up the words, and seal the book until the time of the end; many shall run to and fro, and knowledge shall increase."

Daniel 12:4

The currency of heaven is the spirit of revelation knowledge. Revelation knowledge will be paramount in this last days, and many that will be baptised with the spirit of revelation knowledge will begin to see like Jesus sees and their eyes will be filled with light and perfection.

NOTES

....

....

....

....

....

....

....

....

....

....

....

....

....

....

....

....

....

....

Chapter Nine
The Spirit of Counsel

"Without counsel, purposes are defeated, but in the multitude of counsellors purposes are established."

Proverbs 15:22

"You will guide me with your counsel and afterward receive me to glory."

Psalm 73:24

The spirit of counsel is the spirit of God that gives right judgement. The spirit of counsel enables you to operate on the throne because righteousness and justice are the foundations of the throne. Jesus attained the throne by the spirit of counsel and the fullness of the seven Spirits of God.

The spirit of counsel enables you to perceive things in the spirit and navigate the highest level in the realm of the spirit. The spirit of counsel enables you to understand the deep things of God and perceive the mind of Christ.

"Counsel in the heart of man is like deep water, But a man of understanding will draw it out"

Proverbs 20:5

The Spirit of Counsel prepares us for position. It teaches us how to access the counsel of God, resolve issues and commune with God about the operations in the throne room of God, his advisors, the Trinity and their role in our lives and how to reign and subdue the kingdoms of darkness and dominate the earth to the glory of God's name.

The Lord God is the one that is great in counsel and mighty to execute His counsel in the right time and season. The baptism of the spirit of counsel enables you to have a clear knowledge of the secrets of God and receive clear counsel from the word of God through the Holy Spirit.

Effective prayers is by counsel from the word of the Lord revealed through the Holy Spirit, the spirit of truth. The Holy Spirit is the spirit of counsel.

When you are baptised with the spirit of counsel, you will have the ability to take hold of the truth of the word of God and use it effectively to offer solutions to every life- and societal problem and challenge.

You are bound to wage a good warfare and attain victory through the baptism of the spirit of counsel and wisdom.

> *"Plans are established by counsel; By wise counsel wage war"*
>
> ### *Proverbs 20:18*

The baptism of the spirit of counsel is the spirit of strong guidance. Wise counsel will enable you to make wise decisions and choose right at every point in life. Your steps will be ordered by the Lord in the right direction. Your words will bring right guidance to people around you and you will have a positive influence in people's lives to the glory of God.

Interpretation of Dreams by the Spirit of Counsels

The baptism of the Spirit of Counsel enables you to interpret dreams accurately according to the mind of Christ. Daniel interpreted King Nebuchadnezzar's dream accurately because he was baptized with the 7 Spirits of God. Joseph was also baptized with the Spirit of Counsel inside the prison, he stood out and was able to solve the problems of the nation because Joseph was filled with the Spirit of Counsel. Genesis 39:20

Little wonder why royal kings on the earth surround themselves oftentimes on their Thrones with wise counselors and their Thrones is established in righteousness.

"The counsel of the Lord stands forever, the plans of His heart to all generations."

Psalm 33:11

"Listen to counsel and receive instruction, that you may be wise in your latter days."

Proverbs 19:20

The Lord God leads by wise counsel. The baptism of the spirit of counsel makes you wise and not foolish. It is through the counsel of God by the Holy Spirit that you wage victorious warfare. The devil cannot fault God's counsel, neither will he understand the counsel in the heart of God. The counsel of God stands forever and cannot be refuted.

The baptism of the Spirit of Counsel to know God's will

The baptism of the spirit of counsel leads and guides you into God's sovereign will. Worldly and fleshly counsel leads to confusion, destruction and death eventually. The spirit of God's counsel, which is the spirit of truth, leads you into all truth and guides you in the path of righteousness to do the will of God and fulfill His eternal Kingdom purpose on earth.

NOTES

....

....

....

....

....

....

....

....

....

....

....

....

....

....

....

....

....

....

....

Chapter Ten
The Spirit of Might

"That you may walk worthy of the Lord, fully pleasing Him, being fruitful in every good work and increasing in the knowledge of God; strengthened with all might, according to His glorious power, for all patience and longsuffering with joy."

Colossians 1:10-11

God Almighty takes pleasure in us when we depend wholly upon His strength and not our own strength. He wants His strength to become a reality in our daily lives. Being baptised with the spirit of might means to exchange your weaknesses for God's strength. The strength and power of God changes everything in us for good.

The baptism of God's might and power will empower you to become a supernatural being, created for signs and wonders. Through the baptism of the spirit of might and power, the glory of God is made manifest fully in your life with glorious liberty, as you will become kingdom solution provider in a chaotic world.

God is all-powerful. He is full of strength, might and power. Because we are created in His own image and His likeness with His characteristics and attributes, He wants us to rule, reign, subdue the kingdom of darkness and dominate the earth through His power and strength to His glory.

The baptism of the spirit of might enables you to engage in spiritual warfare and be a victorious warrior through the power and delegated authority of God with His might. The God of Israel is He that gives power and strength to His people.

> *"All authority has been given to me in Heaven and on earth, go ye into the uttermost part of the earth and make disciples of all Nations. Behold, I am with you till the close of age".*
>
> ### Matthew 28:18
>
> *"....They that know their God, they shall be strong and do exploit"*
>
> ### Daniel 11:32

The baptism of the spirit of might, brings forth spiritual breakthroughs with great expansion that destroys limitations and enables you to run distances without measure for God and achieve great exploits with informed revelation knowledge and without getting weary.

The baptism of the spirit of might give inner strength to wait on God patiently until He makes all things beautiful for you in His own time and gives you strength.

The apostle Paul prayed for the church at Colossae, that they would be "strengthened with all power, according to his glorious might, for all endurance and *patience*".

Patience is the evidence of inner strength. Impatient people are weak and therefore dependent on external supports, like schedules that go just right and circumstances that support their fragile hearts. Their outbursts of oaths and threats and harsh criticisms of the culprits who crossed their plans do not sound weak, but that noise is a camouflage for their weakness.

Patience demands tremendous inner strength that can only come from God. That is why Paul prayed for the Colossians. He asked God to empower them for the patient, and endurance that the Christian life requires. But when he says that the strength of patience is "according to God's glorious might", he doesn't just mean that it takes divine power to make a person patient. He means that faith in this "glorious might" is the channel through which the power for patience comes.

> *"It is God who arms me with strength, and makes my way perfect. He makes my feet like the feet of deer, and sets me on my high places. He teaches my hands to make war, so that my arms can bend a bow of bronze."*
>
> **Psalm 18:32-34**

The baptism of the spirit of might leads you by the light of His seven eyes to make your ways perfect and to walk in perfect direction.

The baptism of the spirit of might and power enables you to be courageous and resilient, never to give up at any point in time – even in the middle of the storm.

The baptism of the spirit of might releases a supernatural anointing upon you to soar and live to perform signs and wonders on earth to the glory of God's name.

The baptism of the spirit of might releases the seven horns' anointing upon you that makes you fearless, bold, and strong, and to become irresistible and unstoppable without limitations.

The baptism of the spirit of might makes you successful when everyone else has fallen. The spirit of might makes you dynamic and bold to operate on the throne as a mighty warrior.

Samson was baptised with the spirit of might and he was able to lift the pillars upon the Philistines and destroyed many enemies of God in a day without his physical eyesight. The spirit of might enabled Samson to break barriers.

The weapons of our warfare are not carnal, but they are mighty through God in the pulling down of strongholds. The spirit of might enables believers in Christ Jesus to exercise their spiritual authority and utilise the power that works inside of us to pull down all strongholds of the enemy and dominate our Kingdom inheritance to the glory of God's name on earth.

Jesus Christ was baptised with the spirit of might and He was made strong – even inside the grave. He prevailed and ruthlessly destroyed the power of the grave!

The baptism of the spirit of might enabled Esther to possess the gates of her enemy. She was able to labour in the place of uninterrupted intercession that destroyed the enemies of the people of God, and possessed the nation as their inheritance.

When the spirit of might came upon the Israelites after they entered the Promised Land, they brought down the walls of Jericho with strength and power from the God of Israel.

> *"Arise and shine for your light has come and the glory of the Lord is risen upon you".*
>
> ### Isaiah 60:1

The spirit of might give grace that releases power to arise and push back the darkness that covers your heart, mind, psyche and have victory over people that hinder the manifestation of God's glory on earth at the right time and right season.

> *"The spirit of the Lord is upon me, because the Lord has anointed me to preach good tidings to the poor; He has sent me to heal the brokenhearted, to proclaim liberty to the captives, and the opening of the prison to those who are bound."*

Isaiah 61:1-2

The baptism of the spirit of might and power enables you to set the captives free, to proclaim liberty to the captives and subdue the kingdom of darkness that dominates people's lives from generation to generation because of sin and iniquity.

The baptism of the spirit of might enables us to operate on the throne with heavenly hosts in the court of heaven that surrounds the throne of mercy.

It is imperative to ask the Lord for the baptism of the fullness of the spirit of might in these last days, to exercise dominion upon your thrones on the earth, to rule, reign over and subdue all other kingdom of darkness, principalities and powers in high places and establish the Kingdom of God and His will in our territories and nations.

The spirit of might sets boundaries

David received the baptism of the spirit of might and was able to set boundaries for the Philistines. He stopped the roaring of Goliath and delivered the Israelites from the bondage and captivity of Goliath, the uncircumcised Philistine.

We are called as kings and priests to reign on the earth to the glory of God. The baptism of the spirit of might teaches and empowers us to do the work of God and fulfill our

Kingdom destiny and finish well, as it is written in the book concerning us.

Strategic Prayer Counsel

1) Lord, baptise me with the fullness of the spirit of might with the seven horns' anointing to fulfill my Kingdom purpose and finish well.
2) Lord, baptise me with the spirit of might to be courageous.
3) Lord, baptise me with the spirit of might and power to execute your counsel as it is written in the book concerning me on earth in Jesus' powerful name.

NOTES

....
....
....
....
....
....
....
....
....
....
....
....
....
....
....
....
....
....

Chapter Eleven

The Spirit of the Fear of God

"The secret of the Lord is with those who fear Him.
And He will show them His covenant"
Psalm 25:12-14

The spirit of the fear of God is the spirit of worship in awe of Him, in truth and in the fear of God Almighty. The spirit of the fear of God is the spirit of humility.

God establishes a covenant relationship only with those who fear Him. He gives them divine direction, instruction and counsel. He gives them light and perfection in order not to stumble but to choose right and abhor evil. He reveals deep secrets to them. He gives them the hidden riches and the treasure of darkness to dwell in prosperity.

He releases unto them a godly inheritance in perpetuity to their children's children! He shows them His mercy and fights their battles (Psalm 118:4-6). He gives them divine wisdom – not corrupt, worldly wisdom.

He gives them a personal Angelic Security Guard to keep them save wherever they may go on the surface of the planet. He who fears God and is baptised with the spirit of the fear of God will not be afraid of any storm, because God is present there (Psalm 34:7-10).

The baptism of the spirit of the fear of God enables you to receive deep revelation of mysteries from the heart of the Lord. His thoughts can only be revealed by the fullness of the spirit of the fear of God.

The baptism of the spirit of the fear of God unlocks your Kingdom destiny and gives right direction to fulfill your destiny on earth according to God's will and begin to operate at the throne of mercy.

> *"And I say to you, My friends, do not be afraid of those who kill the body, and after that have no more that they can do. But I will show you whom you should fear; fear Him who, after He has killed, has power to cast into hell; yes, I say to you fear Him!"*
>
> ### Luke 12:4-5

Mordechai was baptised with the spirit of the fear of God. He was controlled, directed and led by the spirit of the fear of God and it enabled him to do the right thing at the right time to gain victory and give God pleasure. He was not ruled by the fear of men, he set his face like a flint and was unflinching by the fear of man. He stood for the cause of God's Kingdom purpose and the whole agenda of the Kingdom.

The baptism of the fear of God enables you to have deep intimacy with God and to know what is burning in the heart of

God. It gives you a high level of discernment, wisdom, humility, holiness and boldness like a lion.

The baptism of the spirit of the fear of God enables you to have clear spiritual sight to see the plans of the enemy and not to fear the enemy but to expose the works of darkness with boldness and command the light to shine. The baptism of the spirit of the fear of God upon your life enables you to generate light that dispels darkness wherever you are.

The baptism of the spirit of the fear of God enables you to understand God's time and seasons and to cooperate with Him to restore His Kingdom glory and to advance the Kingdom of God on earth by His manifold Throne grace.

There is a measure of throne grace that is released upon you when you are baptised with the Spirit of the fear of God to overcome all forms of noisesome pestilences on the earth.

Daniel was baptised with the spirit of the fear of God and was able to cooperate with God to advance His Kingdom agenda. He was unflinching in his faith and was able to stand against all the plans of the enemy and advance God's plan in his generation.

The baptism of the fear of God enables you to use your spiritual authority with boldness to exercise justice over the enemy of God, enforce the will of God's Kingdom on earth and bring generational transformation as it is being done in heaven.

The baptism of the spirit of the fear of God brings you to the place of complete obedience and surrender to the will of God without compromising your stand.

Daniel stood his ground because of the fear of God. He refused to compromise and he was brought to a place of prominence and relevance above all others in his generation and God revealed His deep secrets to him and the mysteries of His Kingdom afterwards.

"The fear of the Lord is clean, enduring forever, the judgement of the Lord are true and righteous altogether, more to be desired are they than gold, Yea, than much fine gold; sweeter also than honey and the honeycomb. Moreover by them your servant is warned, and in keeping them there is great reward"

Psalm 19:9-11

The baptism of the fear of God brings you to a place of safety and access to the mercy of God from the throne of mercy.

"But the mercy of the Lord is from everlasting to everlasting on those who fear Him, and His righteousness to children's children."

Psalm 103:7

The baptism of the spirit of the fear of God enables you to be zealous for the glory of God. It enables you to run away from all sins and iniquities and shake off anything that may hinder you from manifesting the glory of God.

Joseph was baptised with the spirit of the fear of God and ran away from committing fornication with Potiphar's wife and afterwards he was moved from prison to the palace to manifest the glory of God in his generation.

Deep mysteries of God's Kingdom are revealed to those who are baptised with the spirit of the fear of God. It enables you to have a right focus on God's Kingdom agenda above your own will and personal ambition.

The baptism of the spirit of the fear of God enables you to discern people's gifts and callings and help develop, train and mentor them to the full potential God has created them to have on earth. It enables you to lay down your life for others, equip them with spiritual tools and empowerment and release them into the fullness of their Kingdom destinies.

The baptism of the spirit of the fear of God separates you from evil association that can defile your priesthood and corrupt your character. Defilement of priesthood and soiling of your priestly garments will keep you out of God's presence and hinder you from hearing the voice of the Lord as a priest of God.

The baptism of the spirit of the fear of God enables you to set your Kingdom priorities right towards the fulfilment of God's Kingdom mandate.

Strategic Prayer Counsel

1) Lord, baptise me with the Spirit of the Fear of the Lord!
2) Lord, baptise my children with the Spirit of the Fear of the Lord!
3) Lord, baptise our leaders with the Spirit of the Fear of the Lord that your **GLORY** will be restored and fill our land before your second coming!

Seven Steps to Access the 7 Spirits of God

1) Ascertain your salvation and covenant relationship with God. You must be born again (John 3:3).
2) Discover your Kingdom purpose, gifts and calling on earth and be determined and focused to fulfill your destiny on earth (Ephesians 4:7, Ecclesiastes 3:1-2).
3) Seek God diligently with a pure heart and close intimacy with Him and desire to do His pleasure without distractions and compromise (Daniel 11:32).
4) Avoid all distractions and religious traditions that bring deception and false worship (John 4:24).
5) Establish your heart by **GRACE** in God's sovereign will and unite your heart to fear God more than any other thing on earth! Seek to fulfill His Kingdom agenda and not your own agenda. Remember, He relates with you

based on the state of your heart. *"The heart of the matter is the matter of the heart."*

6) Avoid every relationship that works contrary to your kingdom destiny and erodes grace from your life (Psalm 1:1-3). **"Do not be deceived: Evil Company corrupts good habits. 1 Corinthians 15:33**

7) Promptly obey the guidance and instructions of the Holy Spirit. Remember every character fault, sin and iniquity keeps you out of God's presence and hinders you from hearing His voice clearly (John 14:26). Repent and renounce every ancestral faulty foundation and character fault, sin, and iniquity, they keep you out of God's presence and hinders you from hearing God's voice clearly. (Psalm 19:12-14).

It is imperative to study and meditate on the words of God on a daily basis, because all His counsel and instruction comes from His law. It's no wonder that David prayed fifteen times and asked God to teach him and give him understanding regarding His laws. Psalm 119:73-74.

Seven Antidote to Access the Spirit of the Fear of God

"The fear of the LORD is to hate evil; Pride and arrogance and the evil way and the perverse mouth I hate.

1) The Fear of the Lord is to hate Evil
2) The Fear of the Lord is to hate Pride
3) The Fear of the Lord is to hate Arrogance
4) The Fear of the Lord is to hate Crooked ways
5) The Fear of the Lord is to hate Perverse Mouth
6) The fear of the Lord is to hate Wickedness against God and His creator
7) The Fear of the Lord is to hate hypocritical attitude and lifestyle.

NOTES

....
....
....
....
....
....
....
....
....
....
....
....
....
....
....
....
....
....
....

Chapter Twelve

Prophetic Declaration

"Arise and shine; for your light has come! And the glory of the Lord is risen upon you."

Isaiah 60:1

1) The Spirit of the Lord God is upon me. The Lord has anointed me to preach good tidings to the poor.

2) I will break forth and expand to the right and to the left, and my descendants will inherit the nations, and inhabit the desolate cities.

3) I will be made strong for my generation. I have been made a covenant for my people in their generation.

4) I am established in the portion of my inheritance and my cup runs over.

5) The everlasting covenant of the peace of God is established in my life forever.

6) My stones shall be laid with colorful gems, my foundations will be laid with sapphires.

7) The sure mercy of God shall not depart from me and my children's children in their generation.

8) The covenant of the everlasting Priesthood that releases God's kindness shall not depart from me forevermore.

9) I shall be named the priests of the LORD, I shall eat the riches of the Gentiles, and in their glory l shall boast.

10) I will greatly rejoice in the LORD my God, for He has clothed me with the garments of salvation, He has covered me with the robe of righteousness and now my GLORY will awake!

AMEN!

About the authors

Apostle Gbenga and Dr. Janet Adegbenro are servants of God, dedicated mentors, authors and teachers of the word of God with a mandate of restoration of God's kingdom glory on the earth. They are engaged with the restoration of the Priesthood and kingdom authority of believers as kings and Priests with practical applications towards personal, marriage and community transformation.

They are the founder of Global Thrones Ministries and Global Thrones Training Institute, established with the mandate of training and mentoring Thrones Intercessors and kingdom believers with kingdom principles on how to operate on their Thrones and fulfil their God's kingdom mandate on the earth. They are the visionary leader of **Vision 2020 and beyond movement: Operating on the Thrones** – A global movement towards the intentional implementation of strategies and blueprints for enthronement of generations of righteous leaders in all spheres of society.

They are blessed with three prophetic children, Goodness, Mercy, and Peace to the glory of God and they reside in Pretoria, South Africa

Other books written by the authors

1) Rebuilding desolate Foundations
2) Restoration
3) Open Heavens
4) The Mystery of God's Grace
5) The Cross Identity
6) The Power of Kingdom Identity
7) 7 Kingdom Keys and the operating principles
8) Developing Learning Skills
9) The Seven Spirits of God's Workbook (For Supernatural Transformation)
10) Interceding for Kings and Queens
11) 21 Days Prophetic Prayers and Fasting
12) Covenantal Altars
13) 72 Hours Priestly Consecration Prayers and Fasting

www.ingramcontent.com/pod-product-compliance
Lightning Source LLC
LaVergne TN
LVHW051244080426

835513LV00016B/1722